To Jennifer with lo...
Helen Reynolds

your friend,
givan

THE TREASURE OF CHARTER OAK

Ivan, age 14

THE TREASURE
of
CHARTER OAK

*Growing Up in the
Masonic Home for Children
1928-1938*

Ivan Reynolds
with
Helen Ambroff Reynolds

FITHIAN PRESS
Santa Barbara
1989

Dedicated to our son Dr. Bob

"Christmas in the Masonic Home" and "Hearts and Flowers
for Emily" first appeared in *Senior Magazine*.

Library of Congress Cataloging-in-Publication Data

Reynolds, Ivan G., 1921—
Treasure of Charter Oak: Growing up in the Masonic Home for
Children, 1928-1938 / Ivan G. Reynolds & Helen Ambroff Reynolds
Summary: A memoir in which the author describes how he was
raised during the Depression in an orphanage run by the Masons.

ISBN 0-931832-34-9

1. Reynolds, Ivan G., 1921- . 2. Foster children— California—
Biography. 3. Masonic Home for Children (Covina, Calif.)—
History— 20th Century. 4. Group homes for children— California—
Case studies. [1. Reynolds, Ivan G., 1921- . 2. Orphans. 3. Masonic
Home for Children (Covina, Ca.)] I. Reynolds, Helen, 1927- . II. Title.

HV883.C2R49 1989
362.7'32'092—dc20
[B]   89-34633
[92]   CIP/AC

Published by
FITHIAN PRESS
Post Office Box 1525
Santa Barbara, California 93102

THE TREASURE OF CHARTER OAK

PREFACE

My reasons for writing this book are threefold: 1) to express my appreciation to the Free Masons for providing me with food, shelter, and protection, along with excellent values that have lasted a lifetime; 2) to pass on a piece of history that needs to be told; and 3) to come to terms, personally, with the experiences of my childhood.

My sincere thanks are extended to the Masons who, by paying their dues and participating in the development of the Home, touched the lives of so many children. Some served on the Board of Trustees; others came with their lodge members to spend a Sunday, interacting with us, playing softball, sharing a meal. Members of the Monrovia Lodge made sure that we all enjoyed a wonderful Christmas, with their spectacular annual party.

The objectives of the Masonic Home were noble. We were taught the value of work, cooperation, cleanliness, and good manners. What they could not provide, obviously, was our missing normal family. I'm sure they tried; the fact that the institution was called a Home implies that. But the void left by the separation from parents could not be filled by houseparents and other adults in the Home, no matter how hard they may have tried.

With that thought in mind, I wish to point out that the following story is in no way an indictment of the Masons. Rather, it is intended to document the ten years...1928-1938 that I personally experienced in the Home.

I have purposely omitted writing about the girls and their experiences, except where they paralleled the boys'. That story should be written by an author who experienced growing up as a girl in the Home.

It is worthy of note, also, that some of the experiences and events I have described could admittedly be described differently by another participant. This story is my perception and recollection of what transpired. It is interesting that when Home kids get together as adults, individuals remember common events from different points of view.

Special thanks are in order for Mr. John Rose, Administrator of the Masonic Home for Children in Covina. His comments and cooperation have made my task easier.

I am grateful that my wife and sons were able to visit the Home when the old brick buildings stood. They have some idea of the environment that was mine during my years at the Home.

The present situation of the Home is very different from the time I was growing up. The red brick buildings are gone, and in their place are attractive cottages, enabling a much smaller adult- to-child ratio than we had. Today's youngsters have access to counsellors and psychologists. This new concept reflects the modern approach to providing for children who must be separated from their families. Old values, with a modern approach! Clearly, the children are in good hands!

THE TREASURE OF CHARTER OAK

ON TOP OF BUZZARD'S PEAK

It was just about noon when I finally reached the top of Buzzard's Peak. I stood panting under the hot July sun, trying to catch my breath after the steep climb. I meant to plant the crude flag I had carried on the six-mile hike to commemorate my last day in the Masonic Home for Children. I was seventeen years old.

Still huffing and puffing, I managed to dig a small hole, and placed the stick with its white towel into the ground. The wind whipped the cloth mercilessly as I tamped down the dirt around the pole. I wondered if the pennant with my initials could withstand the winds and rains that would come after I'd gone.

Mission accomplished, I took a good look down the mountain, trying to make out the various familiar landmarks that had been a part of my life for the past ten years. There to the left, I could see the town of Covina, laid out neatly on Citrus Avenue. Almost dead center was the Home, with its brick buildings looking like miniature houses in a Monopoly game. Along Garvey Boulevard, tiny cars went about their business, and I could make out the Red Car winding along on what looked like a toy track, probably on its way to Pomona.

Charter Oak Grammer School was barely visible between acres and acres of orange groves. And above everything, looking mighty and haughty, almost opposite Buzzard's Peak, was Mt. Baldy. Even in July, she wore a cap of shimmering snow.

Tears stung my eyes as I took in the view; tomorrow, I would have to leave all of it behind. My friends, the beautiful San Gabriel Valley, Covina High School where I should have spent my senior year...no longer would they be a part of my life.

Yesterday, when I had been called into the superintendent's cottage, I had had no inkling of what was to come. I'd just finished doing some chores on the farm,

9

dressed in a sleeveless shirt and dungarees, because summers in the valley were hot. I'd quickly washed up and brushed stray pieces of hay off my clothes before reporting to Mr. Downen.

"The Old Bear," as some of us boys referred to him in private, was still in his bathrobe, even though it was early afternoon. He looked sour—in fact, downright angry!

I apologized for the state of my clothing, reminding him that I had chosen to work on the farm during summer vacation, instead of accompanying the other kids to the Balboa Island summer Home. He merely grunted, replying that he hadn't called me in to discuss my clothing. As he kept glaring at me, I got up enough nerve to finally ask why I had been called.

"I want you to know that you will be leaving the Home tomorrow," he began.

I was stunned! "You mean I'm being kicked out?"

"If you want to put it that way," he answered.

"But why? What have I done wrong?" I knew that boys were sometimes kicked out, but for serious offenses like disobeying safety rules, smoking, or getting fresh with girls. The only thing I could think of was that I had made some fudge on the hot plate in the chicken shed. I'd been chastised roundly for that by my housemother, Mrs. Bedord.

"Done?" Mr. Downen countered. "You haven't done anything wrong, but your mother certainly has! When Mrs. Knowles, your case worker, called on your mother, she was told to get out and never return. Your mother also told Mrs. Knowles that if her son ever became a Mason, she'd kill him. After all the Masons have done for her, raising five of her children..that's the thanks we get? If that's her attitude, then we do not have to put up with her, nor take care of you any longer!"

"But I have just one more year of school left, Mr. Downen! If I have to live with my mother, I'll need to get a job...and that means I'd have to drop out of school. I don't really know my mother...can't I please stay here for my senior year?

"No", he snapped. "We've been trying to let some of the older children out to make room for young ones who are waiting to get in. That's why Mrs. Knowles went to see your mother...to see if she could possibly care for you. Whether or not she is able to, your mother made the decision for us when she treated Mrs. Knowles so badly. The decision has been made. You leave tomorrow!"

And so it was that on this hot July day in 1938, I awoke early and decided to climb Buzzard' s Peak. Taking in huge breaths of fresh air, I cast one last look at the valley below...my valley with its intoxicating orange blossoms, filled with memories of boyhood dreams.

I hurried down the mountain for the return hike. I would have just enough time to pack my clothes, my letterman's sweater, school annuals, and scrapbooks....the few belongings from my ten years in the Masonic Home.

MY FIRST DAY AT THE MASONIC HOME

May 7, 1928...my sister Julie and I crawled out of the Model T Ford that had stopped in a circular driveway. We had left the Shriner's Home for Children in Redlands, to join our older brothers, Earl and Walter, here. Sister Marie had already left, after spending six years in the Home. I was six years old, soon to be seven, and Julie was eight.

The stranger who had driven us here had not uttered a word on the way. Now he unloaded two battered cardboard boxes that held our worldly belongings and went into the huge, imposing brick building, with us following at his heels.

A prim lady told the man to put the things down, and then dismissed him. Then, without a word to me, she said to Julie, "Come along with me."

I was not to see Julie again, except for a few minutes each day. Girls and boys in the Home only saw each other at meal times, and at school.

Soon, the lady came back and led me to the Junior Boys' Building. She introduced me to the housemother, Mrs. Copeland, and then left.

Mrs. Copeland looked at me with a kind expression, and said, "Come along, Ivan, and I'll show you your dormitory. You will be with some very nice boys about your own age."

"Where are they now?" I asked shyly.

"They're at school, but it won't be long now before they arrive. Why don't you lie down and rest for a while?"

"No, I'm not tired. I want to see my big brother Walter. Is he at school, too?"

When she nodded yes, I told her I wanted to sit outside and wait for Walter...the brother that I had met only once or twice before.

I paced back and forth between the porch and inside the building, checking the old Grandfather clock in the foyer, as if I could really tell time. Where was everybody? And then, finally, I saw a swarm of children approaching...the girls heading for their junior or senior quarters. I studied the taller boys, searching for my seventeen-year-old brother. Mrs. Copeland came out and stood with me. Spotting one little boy, she said, "Oh, Ivan," that boy's name is Walter...is he your brother?"

"No," I said feeling very anxious now, "that's not my brother. My Walter has dark hair and he's very tall!" And just then, the right Walter came running toward me.

He swooped me up and placed me on his shoulders, and piggy-backed me around the grounds, first pointing out the Apple Seed where kids could play marbles or race. He showed me the ball field, Scout House, the hospital, Helps' Cottage, carpenter's shop, and the laundry. Next we skirted the "first forest," and trotted down to the farm. I marveled at the old horse, dairy cows, chickens, and beautiful peacocks. This place was so big, and so different from the Shriner's Home. That had just been a big house.

Walter recited a poem for me as we walked near the citrus trees on our way back to the brick buildings:

Ivan with his little hoe,
To the orchard he would go;
Hoeing weeds here and there,
Til the orchard was all bare!

I giggled, feeling good for the first time all day.

When we reached my building, he squatted down so that he could look directly at me.

"Ivan, I'm glad we can have this little bit of time together. Soon I'll be graduating from high school, and will be leaving here."

It was to be the only time ever...just a few months...that he and I would live in the same place.

Inside my dorm, I faced a dozen boys, all dressed alike in light blue coveralls. I wondered how it was going to be, living with them. I got washed up and got ready for the trip to the dining hall.

Six to a table, plus one adult. Grace was recited by Superintendent Downen, and then we ate. But I can't recall what I ate that first meal; I kept looking around for Julie. She had to be in the same dining room; the older kids were in the adjoining one.

After dinner, before going out to play, I finally spotted Julie. I handed her my favorite marble, asking her to keep it for me. It was a link with my sister that I needed very much that day!

Cleaned up, and clad in identical cotton pajamas, all of us boys took to our iron beds for the night...but I couldn't sleep. It had been a day that would be seared into my memory forever. It was very quiet. I thought I heard the rattling of the electric Red Car making its way along steel tracks...and finally I slept.

CHARTER OAK SCHOOL

Before I knew it, the weekend had passed, and Monday dawned hot and clear for my first day in a new school. Saturday morning had been spent doing chores: dusting and polishing the wood floors of the dorm, sweeping the walks around the junior building, and cleaning the big bathroom with its tile floor and huge bathtub. The afternoon was free for playing on the jungle gym or in the sandbox, or playing marbles in the Apple Seed. And that evening, just before bedtime, everyone took their once-a-week bath.

Sunday had begun with our gathering in the parlor for a Bible story and some singing. My favorite was "Jesus Loves Me."

A noontime dinner was followed by a treat of homemade ice cream churned by some senior boys...and then a light supper of rice with cinnamon and milk, short play period, and off to bed!

I had another sleepless night, and woke up on Monday with a knot in my stomach. At breakfast, I picked at my cereal and toast, I was so nervous. Luckily, Mrs. Copeland didn't make a big deal out of it, even though she saw I was not eating. I just wanted to get to school now, to get it over with. I did not like waiting for the unknown.

A big yellow bus with "Charter Oak Grammar School" painted on it began loading on kids in first through eighth grades; the high school kids boarded the Covina Union High School bus at the same time. I got a window seat on our bus, and we finally began the two-mile trip to Charter Oak School.

On the way, we passed the settlement of Charter Oak...a packing house and a general store with one gas pump, surrounded by oak trees. Jackie, sitting next to me, told me that robbers had buried a treasure map in one of the holes of an oak...and everyone hoped to some day find the map (or charter, as it was called.) I made a mental note to hunt for the charter myself one day. And just then, we pulled up in front of the school.

The buildings were in the shape of a U, with classrooms on either side of an outdoor stage. The office and cafeteria were behind this main building.

My friend Jackie, who was my age and had already been in the Home for three years, showed me to my room, a combination first and second grade class. He introduced me to Miss Shepard, the teacher. When she asked me if I was a first or second grader, I replied, "Second," just as my brother Walter had told me to do. In truth, I had never been in the first grade. I'd just had a few months of kindergarten while in the Shriner's Home.

"All right, Ivan," Miss Shepard said, "Sit over here with the second graders."

By noon, she knew that I should have been placed in first grade, but the kindly Miss Shepard did not shame me in front of the other kids. She let me stay in my section of the room, knowing full well that I would be sitting there again come fall.

By noon, I was smitten with a golden-haired, blue-eyed angel named Emily. She was the prettiest girl in the class—no, in the world! On the playground, instead of entering into the various games, I wondered if I would ever have enough nerve to talk to her. Maybe I would be lucky enough to sit near her in the cafeteria tomorrow. All the Home kids sat in one section of the cafeteria, since we got free lunches, and so were segregated.

By the time 2:30 came, I was exhausted and discouraged. I hadn't understood the work, I couldn't read, and I really didn't feel comfortable with my classmates yet.

When we lined up for loading on the bus for the return trip to the Home, I caught Emily looking at me, and she smiled. I couldn't believe it! And to further make my day, she chose to sit beside me on the bus. Some of the older boys began to tease us, saying, "Go on...hold her hand." One didn't disobey the big guys...so I took her hand and held it. Emily, as shy as she was, didn't seem to object. She somehow sensed how lonely and lost I had been all day. After all, the common bond we Home kids had was that one or both of our parents were dead. Emily understood!

As the bus slowly pulled out, I noticed that the sky was very blue, the orange trees were loaded with fruit, and just for a moment, a yellow butterfly lit on my window. It was a good day, after all! I was going to make it through.

MY FIRST SUMMER

After school let out in June, all I could hear from the "old-timers" was: "We're going to Bal!"
"What's Bal?" I asked. And one of the older kids explained that the word was short for Balboa, an island about an hour and a half drive away, and on Balboa Island was the Home's summer camp.

"It's a lot of fun," my mentor added. "You can swim, go fishing, ride the ferry boat to the mainland, or just make castles in the sand." I began to catch "Balboa Fever" myself.

But that excitement soon gave way to fear and apprehension when I was told that all newcomers had to have their tonsils taken out. I remember saying to the Nurse: "But I feel okay. Why do I have to have an operation?" The nurse, without blinking an eye, shot back: "Because it's policy!"

Woe, woe...an operation! Who else, I wondered, was doomed. I asked around, and sure enough all the new arrivals aged six and seven, sometimes older, boys and girls alike, were to be taken to Covina Hospital for tonsilectomies.

Remo, a newly-arrived boy in my dorm, was also one of the victims. He and his brother Elbe had come in together, but Elbe was assigned to live in the hospital because of severe asthma. Remo had just gotten used to the idea of being separated from Elbe, and began to relax.... He regaled us with his hilarious Pat and Mike jokes, until Mrs. Copeland would have to come in and hush us. But now, no one was joking or laughing, as we prepared ourselves for the operation we didn't need.

Lined up at the hospital, we were called in, one by one. Remo and I tried in vain to make ourselves invisible. I felt my stomach lurch when the nurse called out IVAN REYNOLDS, and I slowly walked into the operating room. The doctor had me lie down on the table, and a nurse spread cold cream all over my face...and then I began breathing in the sweet-smelling ether.

The next thing I knew I was being lifted into a waiting car, and in a haze, I realized the operation was over. And within a half-hour, I was settled into a bed at the Home hospital for the recovery period. I looked over at the next bed, and Anna Mae, one of my classmates, looked as miserable from her operation as I felt after mine.

A few hours later, that evening, I looked up to see my big brother Walter. He had came to visit me, bringing along a Baby Ruth candy bar. I thanked him, weakly, but it was days before I could eat that candy bar.

Recovery over and restored to normal, I again looked forward to going to Balboa for the summer. Some of the older boys had built wooden chests for their belongings; Remo and I packed our things into sturdy cardboard boxes. We were ready for the long awaited trip to Bal.

This was accomplished with a long caravan of cars driven by volunteer Masons. We piled into our assigned cars, clasping our gear, and excitedly began the trip...over to Pacific Coast Highway, past Newport Beach, and finally to the small island which housed our camp. Our summer Home

stood scrubbed and shiny in the afternoon sunshine, ready for the doings of 185 kids and the numerous adults who would supervise and care for us.

Our summer Home, a cluster of barracks, was situated on the banks of the Old Canal. There, near the bridge, we could see rowboats, canoes, sailboats, and rafts ready for our eager use. We spied a tower, from which some of the more skillful divers would be doing their one-and-a-halfs.

We tumbled out of our cars and made our way to the assigned sleeping quarters—age groups together. After depositing our gear and claiming our bunks, we wandered over to the big recreation barracks called Harmony Hall. This would be the scene of skits and programs. The dining hall and small offices completed the complex.

But it was the water and sandy beach that fascinated us most; and most of our time would be spent in the water, or playing in the sand. The older guys and girls would get to swim in the channel and hike to Rocky Point where they would body surf. They would also be allowed to find jobs on the Mainland if they so desired.

It was that first summer that I learned to swim—right in the canal. And after I had it mastered, I taught Remo what to

do. By summer's end, we would both be able to swim across the canal. One thing we had learned quickly at the Home was that fear and tears were not tolerated; so we kept at a task until it was mastered.

Saturday night skits in Harmony Hall were hilarious. Each week, a different age group put on a show—either a play or an exhibition of talent. I taught myself to juggle three oranges, but was too shy to perform in front of everybody. I thought to myself: "Some day, I'll be so good at juggling that I'll perform here in Harmony Hall, using three light globes. By the time I'm a teenager, I'll do it!" From that time on, it was a common sight to see me walking along juggling tangerines, oranges, and tennis balls.

On Sunday mornings, after breakfast, we would listen to Mother Downen, whom everyone adored, as she read articles from Camp Crumb, the newspaper put together by the older boys and girls. She also told us marvelous stories; one that especially stuck in my mind was called "The House with the Golden Windows." The tale was about two children who looked out across the hills and saw a house with golden windows. They thought it must be much better than their own house and their life, so they set out to find the light-filled house.

Lost and hungry, and wandering in circles, they finally came to the house they were seeking; but lo and behold, when they gazed back from where they had come, they saw their own house—which had golden windows. Mother Downen taught us to value what we had instead of searching for something that did not exist.

The big event of August was Balboa Island's Tournament of Lights. Every kind and size of boat imaginable was decorated with lights, and at nightfall they spilled onto the water in a spectacular display of beauty and creativeness. Our Home's little rowboat won a special prize—a canoe! I found out in ensuing years that the Home Kids *always* won some sort of prize, just for participating.

Summer was coming to an end. We did our final exploring...clear over to Lido Isle, which was owned by actor

Jimmy Cagney. In fact, Mr. Cagney leaned over a railing while I was bobbing about in the water and asked me if the water was cold. The way he smiled, I knew I wasn't in trouble having came to Lido.

What a wonderful summer! I was tanned and relaxed, happy with so many fine friends. One newcomer whom I played with that first stay at Balboa was Billy Brown. Billy had acted in Hollywood in the Our Gang Comedies. He was the one who wore his cap on the side.

I don't know why he and his brother and sister were brought to the home, because he never discussed it. But he was very easy to be around, and fit in right away. What we liked about him was that he was not stuck up because he had acted in the movies.

Before we knew it, it was time to return to Covina. Summer was over! We piled into waiting cars for the trip back to the Home, and a new school year. The big boys had already stacked the bunks, cleaned the floors, and locked up the place until next summer.

We were very subdued on the trip back to the Home.

Kenny and Phil Baker

BACK TO SCHOOL

When the yellow school bus stopped to let us out in front of Charter Oak Grammer school in September, I was grateful that I had spent May and June there previously; it had given me a chance to get aquainted with Miss Shepard, whom I would now have as teacher in the second grade. I knew my way around the site, and already understood the rules of fair play and safety that were expected of us. More importantly, I knew most of the kids in my class— outsiders as well as Home kids.

I was glad that Remo and I were allowed to sit next to each other, in our sturdy, wooden desks which were attached to each other in long rows. Remo's first language had been Italian, and sometimes he needed help with the directions the teacher gave. (His English would get better and better, eventually losing all traces of an Italian accent.) Miss Shepard never objected when I would lean across the aisle to help Remo on a work paper.

Learning to read was my biggest challenge, since I hadn't had any beginning instruction to speak of; but I soon began making sense out of the odd-looking symbols that made up words and sentences. Miss Shepard was very patient with my clumsy efforts to read a story or to form the letters of the alphabet.

Miss Shepard also helped me deal with my competitive nature, which often erupted into fights; she encouraged me to channel my energy and anger into physical games and sports. She commented on how fast I could run, planting the seed of confidence that would someday lead to accomplishments in track and field.

CHRISTMAS, 1928

I will never forget my first Christmas in the Home. In fact, nothing before or after could match it, for the Christmas when I was seven left indelible memories and details unmatched by any other holiday.

That Christmas came during fairly good times in the outside world; the crash of '29 and the Great Depression were still in the future. So it was that our housemother informed us we would be able to select one gift out of the Sears catalog, costing up to $3.00. That would be the gift that we would find wrapped under the tree on Christmas morning.

Catalogs were distributed in November, right after Thanksgiving, and the search began. Whenever we could get our hands on the book, we savored the pictures of toys, books and games. We admired the clothes, but no one even considered the clothing. The catalogs became dog-eared, and sometimes accidentally torn, as the deadline for ordering approached.

Finally, I selected a metal train that ran on a small track, when it was wound with a key. The train was set to go under a tunnel through metal mountains. It was colored mostly green—the train, tunnel, and trees that were painted on the mountains.

Now the two biggest Christmas events for us were the Big Party put on for us by the Monrovia Masonic Lodge the weekend before Christmas and then Christmas Day at the Home. But the Monrovia party was the most exciting; we could hardly contain ourselves as we readied ourselves to make the car caravan to Monrovia, twenty miles away.

Scrubbed up and dressed in our Sunday best, we all waited in the early evening air to enter the scores of cars which were lined up in the circular driveway to take us first to the Fox Theater in Monrovia, where we would be treated to a movie.

Finally in my assigned car, sitting in the back seat next to the window, I lifted myself as tall as possible so as not to miss a single thing. It was now totally dark outside, and the motorcycle police who were our escorts used their red lights and blew their sirens as they gunned their way up and down the lineup of cars. Then slowly, very slowly, the caravan began to move.

Along Badillo Street we went with our motorcycle escorts paving the way. Traffic had to stop for us, even if we had the red light, so that we could keep the caravan moving, and the Home kids together. The old Red Car line, running parallel to the road, soon became a race track: the trolley came alongside, then zoomed past us into the night.

By this time we'd arrived in downtown Monrovia, and one by one, the cars stopped in front of the beautiful Fox Theater, discharging their excited cargo. The theater had been rented by the Masons just for us. When we finally took our seats, the lights dimmed, the layers of multi-colored curtains parted, and on the screen appeared Laurel and Hardy. Our individual cares and problems, fears and tragic circumstances were momentarily forgotten as the wild and funny antics of Laurel and Hardy kept us in stitches.

The movie was followed by several cartoons. We lost ourselves in the world of fantasy in this huge, carpeted, magic place!

When the movies were finished, we marched out, row by row, back to the waiting cars that would transport us to the Lodge.

Soon, the Masonic Temple loomed before us, and we got out of the cars, lined up, then quietly entered the lodge room. A magic quiet enveloped us; the place looked like fairyland. The huge ceiling-high tree was ablaze with colored lights; everywhere were garlands of red and green holly, with sparkling angels floating on clouds. All we could do was stare at the mounds of wrapped gifts. Each of us was wondering: "Which one is mine?"

THE TREASURE OF CHARTER OAK

Because I had been raised first in different people's homes, then in the Shriners' Children's Home before coming to the Covina Home, there were no memories of family Christmases—the traditions, gifts, and feasts that happened in normal homes. That's why this Christmas was so astounding for me, with details that would be imprinted in my mind for forever.

Seated in a semicircle around the tree, the little children in front and the bigger ones in the back, tier by tier, we sang carols, sounding like angels. Naughty little boys and mischievous little girls had been transformed by Christmas.

As we were finishing a rousing "Jingle Bells," Santa Claus in all his red and white glory ho-ho-ho'ed his way into the lodge, and we cheered!

"Hello, boys and girls," he shouted with his deep voice. "Have you been good this year?"

A roaring YES! came back.

"Well then, I know that there will be a gift for each one of you. Let me see...who is first?" The calling out of names began...and I waited to hear mine.

When Santa finally called out IVAN REYNOLDS, I fairly flew to him, and everyone laughed because the package he put into my arms was almost as high as I was. I pulled my treasure back to my seat and tore open the red and green wrapping...and to my delight, I saw a large metal airplane, complete with rubber tires, a gift that I would cherish for months to come!

When all the names had been called and the gifts opened, we made our way into the lodge dining room, where each of us was handed a steaming mug of hot chocolate. These were consumed along with decorated cookies—stars, trees, and Santas sparkling with colored sugar.

Before leaving, we again gathered in the lodge room to receive our final delight, a stocking full of candies and nuts. These we would savor, trading "hardies" for "softies," and vice versa. We'd put the nuts into the "softies" and create our own kind of candy. We'd become deliciously sticky with the "hardies," sneaking them into bed at night. It had been quite a party!

Then finally, Christmas Day itself arrived. I remember racing down with the others, into the parlor to our own tree. And there we found the gifts that we had ordered from the Sears catalog. My metal wind-up train with its green tunnel and mountains was as wonderful as it had been pictured in the catalog.

The day was spent playing with our toys and sharing them with our special friends. Some kids eyed others' treasures, wishing they had ordered differently; but I was satisfied. I felt rich, having a wind-up train and the big airplane from the Monrovia Lodge party.

That night, filled with turkey and pie, I snuggled down under the covers of my bed and relived the wonderful past days. I touched my airplane which was on the floor next to my bed, and just before dropping off to sleep, thought: *What an exciting day! What a special Christmas!*

HEARTS AND FLOWERS FOR EMILY

Valentine's Day that first year in the Home took second place only to Christmas. It was a time when one could express love without being teased, because most cards were signed only with a question mark.

All children, regardless of where they are brought up, need love. But as nice as my housemother and teacher were, there was no way that they could love one individual as a parent in a normal home might.

From the first day at Charter Oak, I was smitten with tow-headed, blue-eyed, shy Emily. I still thought she was the prettiest girl I had ever seen; but we never got to see each other at the Home, except once in a while at our assigned dining room table. She was a goddess I worshipped in class, but I dared not let my feelings be known for fear of merciless teasing.

My opportunity to express my admiration for Emily came with Valentine's Day, making the occasion an especially important one for me.

In class, we all made valentines, using red, pink, and white construction paper, cutting out hearts, and fashioning lace with dull scissors.

Most of the boys and girls in our classroom put their favorite friends' names on the valentines, adding the inevitable "from?" And that's how I signed my prettiest valentine for Emily. But that was not enough...I had to do something special to let her know what she meant to me.

Remembering a recent class art project, I asked Miss Shepard if she had an old jar that I could have. She searched around in the cloakroom and soon handed me a quart-size Mason jar. Secretly, I drew some flowers and hearts on paper, then pasted the drawing right on the jar.

After our class party, I carried the jar-turned-vase carefully to the school bus, keeping it well hidden.

Just before dark, I picked a few of the pretty flowers that surrounded our building, and placed them in the vase.

As darkness approached, I crossed over on the pergola, and, with my treasure in hand, went to the junior girls' building. I tapped gently on Emily's dorm window and called out her name; then I jumped in surprise when SHE opened the window. I put the jar into her hands, said, "This is for you," and immediately turned and ran into the dark, straight to my building before anyone could discover what I had done.

What I learned that night was the pleasure of giving to others. I had reached out to express what I considered to be love. I realized that one can express feelings—if not with words, then with deeds.

Nothing came of young infatuation with Emily, of course. We continued to live on opposite sides of the Home, rarely speaking or playing together at school. But the surprised and pleased look on her face when I gave her the "vase" filled with flowers made a lasting imprint on my heart!

THE MYSTERIOUS DISAPPEARANCE OF THE HORN

Shortly after I entered the Home, Remo and Phil came in; I really liked them and felt comfortable around them. That first summer in Balboa had given us a chance to really know each other and become fast friends. And then, in the spring of 1929, a three-year-old was brought in...an orphan, we were told, with nowhere else to go.

His name was Franz, a pitiful looking kid, very skinny, with black hair and soulful brown eyes. Even his face was long, adding to his doleful look.

Everyone felt sorry for "Frank," as the housemother dubbed him; but to me, he became Franzo, and I did what I could to help him fit into the group of much older boys. We, who were three to five years older, were expected to make allowances for Franzo, and to be patient with him for the first few days.

Well, patience was one thing, but what happened when Mrs. Copeland got him a toy horn would have tried Job. Each evening, Mrs. Copeland held Franzo on her lap while he 'entertained' us by blowing mercilessly on his horn. We had to clap and say, "Oh, that was good!" Mrs. Copeland, hoping to cheer up the little fellow, and seeing how pleased he was with his horn blowing, encouraged him to play some more.

By the time he had entertained us several evenings in a row, we'd had it! The only ones apparently thrilled with the performances were Franzo and Mrs. Copeland.

Then tragedy struck! Mrs. Copeland called a meeting, and told us the horn had disappeared. We looked at each other, trying to suppress our joy; who could our hero be?

Franzo was whimpering, "I want my horn" over and over again. We were sent to scour the building, inside and out, to find the horn; but nowhere was it to be found.

I suggested that Franzo take up singing or dancing, but he would have no part of it;he fancied himself a horn player. Now, he had to be content to sit in Mrs. Copeland's lap for storytime, instead of giving us a concert.

And the rest of us, with our ears finally at rest from the blast of the horn, felt a new appreciation for story time. We also treated Franzo especially well.

No one would ever admit taking the horn, but one day it was found all mangled and twisted. In keeping with our code of never telling on each other, we'd each promised to keep the secret, if only the horn-napper would confess. But no one did. Too bad, because whoever was the culprit would have forever been a hero in our eyes!

A MOST UNUSUAL MOTHER

On Mother's Day, each child was given a carnation to wear...a red one for living mothers, and a white one for moms who had died. I wore a red one.

At the time, I knew very little about my mother. Once in a great while, she would come out to visit Julie and me; and a couple of times we went to visit her, wherever she happened to be living at the time. Usually she stayed in a run-down court in Los Angeles; one time, she lived atop Angel's Flight, a landmark in downtown L.A.

Nothing about her conveyed the fact that she had been brought up by a wealthy father, was well traveled, and had received a good education. I was to find out about her background much later, when I sat down with her as an adult.

May Hanson, the eldest of four children, was born in Concordia, Kansas in 1879. Her father, Hans, and mother, Ida, both Swedish, were gentle and loving parents. Hans Hanson owned the entire main block of Concordia, and was looked up to by all the merchants and farmers of the area.

When Mother was just a little girl, the notorious Younger Brothers rode into Concordia, threatening to rob and pillage the town. In an effort to save his town, Hans invited the outlaws into his lovely Victorian home, where they sat down to supper with the family. My mother chatted amiably with the men, regaling them with childish tales. The Youngers spent the night there, and left the next morning without having robbed the bank or firing a shot.

When the Indian Territory of Oklahoma was opened up to settlers, Mother was ten years old. She sat with her father in their horse-drawn buggy, as they waited along with hundreds of others for the signal to begin the Land Rush. Hans lay claim to vast acreage in what was called Cimmeron.

Ida Hanson died bearing her fourth child; she was only 29 years old. Grief-stricken, Hans fell into a deep depression, losing interest in home and business. Leaving the three younger children with a nurse and servants, he took May with him, traveling all over the states and territories. Mother witnessed train stops that bustled with fur traders, Indians, and fortune seekers. Together, father and daughter made it out to California. For a while, they lived at the then brand-new Coronado Hotel in San Diego. My mother fell in love with California.

Upon returning to Kansas, my mother, now a teenager, was sent to a music conservatory in Topeka. There she became part of an all-girl softball team called The Bloomer Girls. The girls' uniforms consisted of daring sleeveless tops and knee-length bloomers.

As a young woman, Mother moved out to San Francisco; she was there during the 1906 earthquake.

Eventually she married and had five children; but she never was domesticated. She once told me with relish how she tried to trick her husband into thinking that she had actually baked a cake. What she had done was to buy a sponge cake and frosted it. My father had been elated until he accidentally found the wrapping of the store-bought cake.

When my father died three months before I was born, my mother was neither equipped to earn a living nor emotionally able to care for her children. They were put into the Masonic Home, all except Julie and myself. Julie stayed with Mother but I was cared for by different people. Then both of us were put into the Shriners' Home, and finally into the Covina Home.

Lying awake many nights, trying to figure out why I hadn't been able to have a normal upbringing, I knew that I loved my mother. Still, there was no closeness between us. She was still pursuing happiness for herself; and she rationalized putting her children into a Home by telling herself that her husband had been a Mason, and had paid his dues toward the Home, and so her children were entitled to live there.

What she couldn't have understood was the emptiness that lay inside me. I yearned for something that I hadn't gotten and never would—a mother's loving care.

Actually, I didn't enjoy her visits to the Home. One time when my brother Earl brought her to see Julie and me, she took some tangerines off the trees; Julie and I were fined $1.00 each out of our accounts for the tangerines. We began to wish that Mother wouldn't bother coming to see us.

We didn't care to go visit her, either. It seemed as though there was always some kind of problem brewing that had her so upset. So, as I lay awake, I'd come to the conclusion that it was a good thing that I had been placed in the Home. I realized that Mother was just not able to maintain a home for her children.

Earl and Walter Reynolds, 1921

THE GREAT DEPRESSION...AND THE KIDS KEEP COMING IN

As hard times in the country became desperate times, more and more kids came streaming into the Home. Johnny, Botch, the Walline brothers, Ed and Bob Ridell, Joe, Alva and the other Nelsons, and Ernest Lidell arrived because of varying circumstances. We would later learn that the four Bayer children lost their father, a motorcycle policeman, as he tried to apprehend some lawbreakers. His story was featured on radio's "Calling All Cars," a popular program during the 1930's.

At one point, the Home became so crowded that some of the children were assigned to live in the hospital.

Our Christmas gifts from the Sears catalog had to be limited to a cost of $1.00...and one year even that was not allowed. The only gifts that kids got were from relatives.

I don't know why, but that Christmas morning Franzo and I were the only ones who received nothing at all. Seeing how upset we were, our housemother took us into her room, and from the dresser she took down two miniature monkey figurines. We each got a monkey; and we tried to act happy with our gifts.

Even the Monrovia party reflected the change: no movie theater was rented just for us, and the gifts were not as expensive or elaborate.

As young as we were, we became aware that Americans were losing their jobs, banks were closing, and people were unable to keep their homes because they couldn't make their mortgage payments. We were really lucky to be fed and sheltered in the Masonic Home, especially during those hard times brought on by the Great Depression.

In most cases, we Home kids came from situations where either the dad had died, leaving the mother financially unable to care for her children, or the surviving dad found it impossible to work and take care of the children. Sometimes children came because a parent was extremely ill, and still others came as orphans.

That was the case of one of the newcomers, a handsome boy named Jack who had lost both parents. Ordinarily, we didn't probe for answers regarding the new kids' circumstances, but somehow we found out that Jack had two uncles who ran fishing boats for Chicken-of-the-Sea Tuna, out of San Pedro. The uncles brought Jack to the Home because his dad had been a Mason, not because he was poor. As it worked out, Jack was able to spend some summers with his uncles, fishing for tuna.

None of us resented Jack, who seemed to have such privileges. Instead, we admired this smart and polite boy, who made most of us look really rough. There was something very special about Jack, and none of us would be surprised when he eventually graduated from Harvard and headed Proctor and Gamble in the East.

But now, he was a new boy in the Home, and was treated as such. Most of us had nicknames of one kind or another. Usually, it was the older boys who dubbed the younger ones with some sort of silly handle that stuck. (Alva Nelson was called "Goofy" because he tinkered all the time.) In Jack's case, knowing that he had come from San Pedro, an older boy announced that that's where the "bug house" was. So over and over again, he asked Jack: "Where do you come from?" When Jack would answer, "San Pedro," the big guy would counter with, "That's where the bug house is. Now, where do you come from?" And finally, Jack replied, in order to hush him up, "From the bug house." And thus Jack became "Bugs."

I figured that nickname was just one notch better than mine: "Spit"! That evolved from the saying: Ivan Skavinsky Skavar, Could spit whiskey so far.

Fortunately, "Spit" gave way to "Ivanich" when I entered high school, just as Jack shed the name Bugs.

But back to the depression. Even as the Home kept receiving more and more children, so did Charter Oak

School. Home kids outnumbered Outsiders three to one. School was the only time we mixed with each other, and even then, Home kids tended to group among themselves outside at play.

The interesting thing was that some of the Outsiders were well-to-do, being children of old-time Covina ranchers. The Burk brothers, from a ranch adjacent to the Home, were driven to Charter Oak by a chauffeur. On the other hand, other Outsiders were poor, coming from families who labored for the ranchers. Lucky White, in my class, came to school without shoes. I envied his freedom as he ran around barefooted; the only time we were allowed to go barefoot was at Balboa.

Up through the sixth grade, our teachers were single women. During the depression, as soon as a woman teacher got married, she was automatically dismissed. The idea was to give single women jobs. Miss Cooper, one of the best teachers at Charter Oak, had to leave when she got married. Yet Mr. Boots and Mr. Reynolds, teachers of seventh and eighth grades respectively, were married and were allowed to teach. The reason was that men were expected to care for their families. No one considered this policy discrimination against women.

As classes swelled to thirty and more children, teachers worked harder than ever to help each one of us to learn. I loved art and sports, but I still found reading and writing dull. During class, I would escape dealing with disliked tasks by daydreaming about finding the mysterious oak tree with the charter that would lead me to wealth and happiness.

It was also during the deep depression when Ralph (whom we called Junior) and I were involved in a fascinating scenario. One Sunday, when the Grand Lodge came to visit the Home, one of the members, a farmer, passed by Junior and me and chatted for a while. We sat in our Sunday best, on our good behavior, looking very much alike with our tow heads and blue eyes.

"How would you two like to live on my farm?" he asked.

35

We didn't know what to say, so we just nodded, stiffly. Then we heard the same man ask our housemother if adoptions were allowed. He said he'd like to adopt Junior and Ivan. But the answer was "No." Children were never adopted out of the Masonic home.

Later on, Junior and I fantasized how it would have been living on the farm with the very nice man. We agreed that it would have been swell to have been the only two kids in a regular home. But of course it was just a brief moment. We were Home kids!

9586 Hospital Hall
Masonic Home.

TOUGH BUT VULNERABLE

The title of the song "Laughing on the Outside, Crying on the Inside" would have been an apt description for many of us in the Home.

We were expected to fall into place without question, even if that meant having perfectly good tonsils removed. Though we appeared able to cope, many of us developed symptoms of anxiety which were beyond our control.

My problem was insomnia. During the day, I seemed to be in control of events; but at night, feelings of frustration and loneliness made sleep difficult and fitful.

Other kids' anxieties manifested themselves in different ways. One child rocked himself to sleep every night. At Balboa, where we had bunk beds, both that child and whoever had the other bunk would rock simultaneously.

Another kid walked in his sleep. Not only did he walk around moaning, but he would usually find me and try to crawl into bed with me. He did this both at Bal and at the Home. I asked Mrs. Copeland to explain why he did it, because it scared me. She explained that he was upset and was seeking comfort. "Maybe," she said, "he feels a connection with you."

Some boys would manage to keep their cool for a time, but then would explode, fighting at the drop of a hat. Those who didn't fight would often tease younger boys, or would provoke pals into fighting each other.

Causes of such behavior, including bedwetting, were never sought. Most kids suffering from deep anxiety kept it to themselves. Not only were they too embarrassed to discuss their concerns; often, they denied having a problem.

One boy who came to the Home claimed to have been horsewhipped by his stepmother. He had scars on his back to prove it. Another boy had suffered, not from intentional harm, but from an adult's lack of knowledge. The mustard

37

plaster that his parent had put on his chest had severely burned him, leaving raised scars.

After I talked with Mrs. Copeland about my fears concerning the boy who kept walking in his sleep, I began to understand a little bit about why so many boys acted the way they did. I could see that there were reasons why they behaved in strange ways.

The most difficult thing for me was to learn to cope with bullies. I was scrawny, though wiry, and I decided that I would just have to learn to fight, even though a bully might be taller and heavier than I. Sometimes I won, and sometimes I lost; but I did vow that I would not bully others, and would protect little kids from bullies whenever possible.

I hoped I would be able to hold my own in this place where our food, clothing, and shelter were as good as or better than many American kids had in normal homes, but where one could not find a lap to climb on or a shoulder to cry on. Sometimes, surrounded by scores of people, I felt very lonely.

EXPLORING THE MINES

Why there weren't numbers of accidents and disasters among us kids is beyond me; we were always trying potentially dangerous things in our free time. We weren't supervised by adults during play time; that led some of us to do things that were clearly taboo, feeling almost compelled to confront danger.

I knew that there were abandoned mines just behind the Home's 43 acres; there were featherstone, silver, and sulphur mines. I would listen to the big guys as they told how they sometimes explored those mines...all except the sulphur mine, for obvious reasons.

One Saturday, Franzo and I decided to go see for ourselves. We hiked down to the featherstone mine and went into the musky cavern. It was cool and dark and scary. As we poked around, Franzo asked, "What do they use this stuff for, anyway?" I was proud that I could answer, "For dishes. They make dishes out of this stuff." It paid to keep your eyes and ears open around the older kids; they seemed to know everything!

After groping around in the dark, narrow tunnel a few minutes, we suddenly heard a loud whirring sound that came from the ceiling. Bats!

Franzo, being so much younger than myself, clung to me. I tried to shake him off so I could defend us against the bats that were now swooping down. Turning toward the distant light, we ran. We kept running until we finally reached the entrance, gasping for air, even though the bats had quit their pursuit minutes before.

That night, in the dorm, when we were all supposed to be asleep, I told the other boys about the adventure that Franzo and I had had in the featherstone mine. After I finished, Jackie told us that from time to time bats would actually fly into the dorms.

I'd always had trouble getting to sleep, as long as I could remember, but that night, sleep seemed impossible. I kept visualising those bats flying out of their cave and making straight for my dorm. I listened carefully, but all I could make out was the sound of the boys' breathing. Still, I pulled the covers over my head, just in case!

Lying there, feeling alone and scared, I tried to switch my thinking to something pleasant. I pictured myself hiking all the way up to Buzzard's Peak, the peak that was visible from the Home. But then I remembered the legend about the peak being an Indian burial ground, and thought about the reason why buzzards were said to constantly circle the peak.

My thoughts went back and forth between bats and buzzards. Then I sat up, and like the proverbial person who whistles in the dark, I said to myself: "When I'm older, I'm going to climb Buzzard's Peak." I also made a note to forget about exploring any other mines. And with that, I drifted off to sleep.

UPSTAIRS TO THE INTERMEDIATE DORM

It was lucky for us boys that we got to have a nice housemother like Mrs. Copeland when we were very young. Her patience and kindness were just what we needed to help us after suffering various traumatic circumstances.

When she left, a couple named Mr. and Mrs. Jones took over as houseparents. Mrs. Jones was downstairs with the very young, and Mr. Jones was upstairs with kids aged ten through twelve or thirteen.

I was due to stay downstairs for probably another year, but for some reason unknown to me, Mrs. Jones called a meeting and said one boy was to be sent upstairs. She explained that she had put slips of paper into a hat, one of which would have the word UP written on it. Whoever pulled the slip with UP would be the one to go upstairs.

"Ivan," she said, "you've been here the longest of this group, so you pull first." I reached into the hat and pulled out the UP slip. Mrs. Jones then said, "Well, there's no need to have anyone else pull. Ivan will be the one to go upstairs." I realized that she had rigged this whole thing so that I would have to be under Mr. Jones' supervision upstairs in the Intermediate Dorm. I hadn't given her any trouble, but I figured she thought I might, since I was so active, and always full of ideas.

I joined the boys upstairs, who were in grades 5-8. I was the youngest one there. I liked the boys, but took an immediate dislike to Mr. Jones. He turned out to be quick-tempered, and didn't hesitate to smack us whenever he felt we deserved punishment.

Rules in the Intermediate Dorm were much tougher than in the Junior Boys', and Mr. Jones did not tolerate the breaking of his rules. Instead of being tuned in to the hurts and anxieties that many of us had, he refused to let anyone touch him emotionally.

With no psychologist or counsellor in the Home, it was no wonder that so many of us settled disputes with fisticuffs at the drop of a hat. Fistfighting, wrestling, or just hitting each other in passing served as a release for us when we were outside. Inside, we stiffly tried to avoid offending Mr. Jones in any way, shape, or form.

I really tried staying out of trouble, but I broke a safety rule one day, thinking I wouldn't get caught. What I did was to climb up on the roof of our three-story building, just to see what things looked like from up there. And Mr. Jones found out!

My punishment? First a lecture, which I deserved. But then, Mr. Jones went over and got a man who worked as one of the secretaries in the office to come and witness the real punishment. The secretary, whom people called "Bodie," had a gleeful look on his face as the three of us went into Mr. Jones' office. I was ordered to drop my pants, and while Bodie watched, Mr. Jones spanked my bare bottom with a heavy paddle. Needless to say, it was a very humiliating experience. But despite the humiliation and pain, I did not cry. I wasn't going to give them that satisfaction.

Despite that episode with Mr. Jones, I did like being upstairs. Now, instead of twelve beds to a room, there were only four. This allowed each boy more space to move around and to keep personal belongings straight.

Another plus was that bedtime was a half-hour later than it had been downstairs, and still another bonus was being allowed to play further away from the buildings during free time.

Also, I was now able to wear bib overalls to school, instead of the coveralls. This was a distinct mark of growing up, just as senior boys all wore cords and cotton shirts to school.

As more and more boys kept coming in, and with the hospital in full use for our rooms, our dorm was inspected for possible additional space. I was moved into the linen closet with a newcomer named Mackie. It was strange having two beds in the middle of the floor, surrounded by stacks of linen on huge shelves.

Redheaded Mackie was a quiet boy, who as it turned out, would be in the Home for just one year. He was a victim of infantile paralysis, and wore heavy metal braces on his legs.

At night, I'd help him take off the braces, and again in the morning, we'd struggle together to get them on. Poor Mackie often cried out in the night from cramps in his legs, and I'd get up and rub his legs until the pain subsided.

Since Mackie couldn't run or jump or play like the rest of us, I made sure that he and I could have some quiet times together. And if I'd had any kind of adventure, such as exploring the first forest, I'd tell him about it while we were getting ready for bed.

Because I knew the consequences of being bad, I truly made an affort to toe the line with Mr. Jones. And having Mackie as a roommate helped keep me out of trouble. But when Mackie left, I went back into a regular room in the dorm, and my exuberance for adventure and pushing the limits emerged again.

Instead of letting off steam at the Home, though, I let it all out at school. Nothing terrible—just talking a lot, and out of turn. Consequently, my desk was moved outside where I would spend most of the fourth grade term. There I was ordered to work by myself, refraining from bothering anybody inside. Luckily, my banishment for misbehavior was not reported to the Home.

The funny thing was that I actually liked being outside. It was a rare chance to be all alone, as opposed to always being a part of a group.

Sitting at my desk, I looked out at the orange trees that surrounded the U-shaped school. I'd chuckle at the quail racing in and out of the irrigation ditches. When it rained, I'd sit protected by the overhang, watching drops of water splashing down, bringing a fresh earthy smell that mingled with the aroma of the orange blossoms.

I still found lessons in reading and spelling unenjoyable, but when those assignments were finished, I'd doodle away, drawing quail, orange trees, and birds flying against a blue sky.

My teacher (whose name I cannot remember) doggedly helped me with my basic skills. She'd come out and, stooping over me, would try to encourage me to understand, and to try harder. She also scolded me for doodling so much. But one day, at the end of the school term, she patted my shoulder and said, "Ivan, you're a good artist. Try to keep an interest in drawing. I think it is good that you delight in your surroundings, and are able to put these things down on paper."

So the year wasn't a total loss. A negative situation had become a positive one, in some ways. And, even though I hadn't done well with the basic skills, I became more aware of other abilities. Sketching and drawing would always be an outlet for my perceptions of the world outside myself. Nature held a fascination for me as a child, as it would later, when I became an adult.

TINSEL LAND IN OUR OWN BACK YARD

Movies were one of the joys of our existence. Every Saturday night after supper, we would all gather in the basement to watch the antics of Laurel and Hardy, Harold Lloyd, and Buster Keaton, plus Westerns starring Hoot Gibson, Tom Mix, and Tim McCoy. Once in a while there was a musical; the boys endured the mushy stuff, while the girls swooned over Rudy Valee and Dick Powell.

The earlier films had been silent ones, and older kids would read the captions for the little ones. Later, talkies were featured, and we sat in awe, listening to the voices coming from the figures on the screen.

Once in a while, real movie stars would come to the Home and, after a tour of the premises, would entertain us. Dick Powell, a Mason in the 20th Century Lodge, came a few times and sang for us. Cross-eyed Chester Conklin, a favorite comedian of ours, also paid us a visit, and had us rolling in the aisles. Still later, Walt Disney came to demonstrate his drawing ability; he made sketches of Mickey and Minnie Mouse, Pluto, and Goofy. Each dorm was given one sketch to hang on the wall.

Like most kids, we loved acting out the different parts we saw in the movies. We were fascinated with the adventures and schemes that were acted out by real people.

Then one day we learned that W.C. Fields was making a film close to the Home!

We were told by the houseparents to stay away from the set while they were filming; W.C. Fields, we were told, had no tolerance for "little darlings." And we obeyed. But just as soon as the filming was over, I decided to go find the set. Even though Franzo and I were in separate dorms, we still played together; in fact, he'd follow me wherever I went. So it was natural that he accompany me on my quest.

We started walking on Badillo toward Covina and

headed toward the private boarding school called Cal Prep, not far from Covina. And all of a sudden, there it was! A whole shack made out of balsa wood! Franzo and I, ecstatic at our discovery, went inside, and to our amazement, all the furniture was made of balsa wood. No wonder chairs broke so easily in the movies, when they were smashed over the villain's head!

Our spirits dampened momentarily, with the realization that the movies were not for real...that those villains and heroes were in no danger, as they knocked each other around, smashing chairs over each others' heads. But our disenchantment lasted only until we acknowledged the magic of making fake things seem so real on the screen. The colored water in the whiskey bottles and the celluloid windows, and flimsy furniture were real when we sat in the dark, watching the images on the screen.

Back at the home, Franzo and I were hailed as heroes by the other boys, when we told them about the movie set; they too decided to visit the shack that would soon appear as a sturdy structure in the movie theaters. And the balsa wood shack? It was eventually torn apart by the kids and made into model airplanes. All that remained were a few whiskey bottles, filled with colored water.

THE DENTAL CAPER THAT FAILED

Saturdays were the time when the dentist, Dr. Wilkins, came to the Home to conduct what we considered the chamber of horrors. He was hired by the Masons to come and take care of our teeth. Having a tooth ache usually meant that the tooth would be pulled—and without benefit of a pain killer.

Even big, brave seniors turned into whimpering babes in that dentist's chair, situated in its own little room in our hospital.

Around Wednesday, I'd gone to our nurse because of an awful toothache. She dabbed something on it which helped, so I thought to myself, "Oh, boy...now I won't have to see Dr. Wilkins."

To doubly ensure my salvation, on the following Saturday, I volunteered to be the 25-cents-a-day messenger for Dr. Wilkins. It would be my job to go from building to building, bringing back with me, the "marked victims."

Usually a nine year old wasn't interested in this duty; but I was willing to sacrifice my playtime this particular Saturday. I figured that if I worked with the dentist, I would not have to have him working on my troublesome tooth. All day I scurried back and forth on my appointed rounds; and as late afternoon approached and the last patient had been released, I turned to leave.

"Just a minute, young man," Dr. Wilkins said, as he motioned me into the dreaded chair. "Nurse tells me that you have a bad tooth."

The jig was up! There was no way out! He gave me a looped piece of cord to pull on, while he went about extracting my tooth, and negating my whole caper.

Finally, I climbed out of the chair and stumbled to the door. Blinking back my tears, I made my way up to my dorm, knowing I would not be able to eat supper or go to that evening's western movie.

Needless to say, I never volunteered as messenger for the dentist again. Sometimes, life just wasn't fair!

HOGIE: SUPER BOY SCOUT LEADER

His real name was William Hoogendyk, but to us boys he was fondly called "Hogie." I'm not sure whether Hogie was a Mason or not, but he was very dedicated to helping the Home boys. For years he served as Scout Master, teaching us exciting skills, and more importantly, acting as a great role model for adolescent boys.

A well-to-do and successful business man, he didn't have to donate hours and hours each week with us, but he did. For me, and for many of the other fatherless boys, he was one of the best liked and most influential adults we would ever know.

Hogie owned three packing houses—the one in Charter Oak, plus two others. The citrus industry was the heart of the San Gabriel Valley, and the packing houses went full-tilt, sorting and packing oranges, lemons, and tangerines for shipment to all parts of the United States.

Upon turning twelve, we automatically joined the Boy Scouts under Hogie's kindly leadership. He was someone who accepted each one of us at face value...trusting us, and helping us to see ourselves as good and worthwhile human beings.

I looked forward to donning the hand-me-down uniform each week, and running down to the Scout House to see what Hogie had planned for our troop. Sometimes, we would stick close to the Home, learning how to track animals by their pawprints. We could identify the prints of coyotes, foxes, and squirrels.

On one outing, we went under the White Bridge, into the creek which ran behind the Home, and there we discovered Indian arrowheads and mortars and pestles. Hogie's soft voice carried us back to the times when Indians had inhabited Home property.

Each week he planned something different, keeping our

interest piqued. One evening, we all got to go to his packing house in Charter Oak to learn about packing processes. Instead of boring us with a speech, Hogie let each one of us ride on the conveyor belt as we followed the oranges that were being sorted. What a teacher! He understood how young boys need to be involved and active in a learning process. No wonder we all admired and respected him!

The highlight of our Boy Scout activities was the big overnight in the San Gabriel mountains. For weeks we could talk of nothing else. And finally, we got ready for the trip to the wilderness.

When the big day arrived, we were transported in several cars to the camp grounds. No sooner had we piled out of the cars and camp was being set up, Remo and I, along with a couple of other guys, trotted off by ourselves to see what lay adjacent to our camp. We came to a quick halt when we realized that we'd come to a sharp drop. But there on a nearby tree was a rope, tied onto a branch and hanging down. At the bottom was a perfectly fashioned knot.

Tarzan, in his movies, could not have asked for a more perfect rope to swing from branch to branch. Mimicking the great Johnny Weisemuller, I ran to the rope with both hands, and gave a big push, meaning to swing over the cliff and back. And that's the last thing I remember.

I regained consciousness in Hogie's car, just as we were driving through Covina and heading toward the Home and the hospital. I dazedly mustered up a "What happened?"

Hogie explained that the rope had slipped from my hands, causing me to reel through space and land down the cliffside. Bodie and some of the scouts had helped Hogie carry me through the woods to the awaiting car for the trip back home.

Hogie pulled into the Home's driveway and then stopped in front of the hospital. He gently helped me in, and explained what had happened to the nurse. He made sure that his explanation did not make me sound at fault. When I was settled into a bed, Hogie came in to say goodnight. He told me that he was sorry that I had been hurt; not once did he admonish me for doing something foolish.

Hogie realized that I had already suffered enough, sustaining a concussion. He didn't see the need to lecture me about engaging in any future dangerous stunts.

Words cannot convey my gratefulness to this kind man. He made me proud to be a Boy Scout, and even prouder to count him as a mentor and a friend. With those thoughts, I fell asleep.

A few months later, our troop got ready to take another overnight, this time to Yermo, out in the desert. As usual, there was an air of excitement during the preparation period.

Just before the weekend of the overnight, I got into some sort of trouble with the housefather, and I was told that I couldn't go on the outing. I was disappointed, of course, because I enjoyed being with Hogie whenever possible; but I accepted the consequences of whatever it was that I had done. I watched my dorm mates march on out with all their gear, trying hard not to show my envy.

When they returned on Sunday, the boys all looked haggard and done in; not one of them talked about the outing. Finally my curiosity got the better of me and I asked Ed about the trip. He rolled his eyes upward, and moaned: "YERRRRRRR-MO."

"What do you mean?" I asked.

And all he could say was "Yerrrrr-mo!" The other guys picked up on it and all started in a chorus saying "YERRRRR-MO!"

The stay had been one manifested with extreme heat, mosquitoes, and tracking paw prints in the desert. So the boys, instead of having a great weekend, ended up envying me because I had stayed behind.

After that, all anyone had to say was "Yerrrr-mo" and we'd collapse with laughter. That became the code word for something that was anything but great.

Despite the Yermo fiasco, Hogie continued to be our idol. When he told us that our troop was responsible for providing entertainment for the next Court of Honors, we were all willing to help.

Someone suggested that I do my juggling act. Everyone agreed, since my buddies had all seen me juggling three oranges, lemons, or tennis balls without dropping them.

Hogie asked me if I would be willing to demonstrate my juggling skills at the meeting of all the area troops, and of course, I agreed. How could I refuse Hogie?

I practiced and practiced until I got bored with handling oranges and balls. I decided I'd surprise everyone by doing something spectacular. Secretly, I practiced juggling three light bulbs, working over my bed just in case I should drop one. But I didn't! Not once did I drop a light bulb! I was feeling very confident by the time the Court of Honors was held.

On the evening of the big event, the Scout House in Covina was packed with boys from all over the valley. The meeting started out with the awarding of various merit badges. As the time for the performance segment came closer, I began to get very nervous. Hogie looked over at me, and gave me an encouraging wink.

Then, there it was! The announcement that Ivan Reynolds would juggle was made, and I found myself standing on the little stage. I started my act by juggling tangerines...perfect! And the boys cheered! Next, I changed to tossing and juggling three tennis balls, higher and higher into the air. The applause was deafening.

And then the finale. A hush came over the audience as I displayed three lightbulbs. My heart was thumping, and my palms were sweaty. I put the bulbs down for a moment while I wiped my hands on my tan scout trousers. Then, I picked up the light bulbs again.

Up went the first one, followed by the second, but before I could toss the third one up, the first two had come splintering down to the hard floor. With the third bulb still in my hand, I stood frozen. My finale was a disaster.

Everyone remained quiet while one of the Scout Masters came up on the stage to help clean up the shattered glass. I prayed for an earthquake so that I could be swallowed up and out of sight. But not even Mother Nature was going to get me out of this embarrassment.

I went back into the audience and sat down. The program continued with other acts, which, frankly, I don't remember. What I do recall is that all of a sudden, there was a gentle hand placed on my shoulder, followed by a couple of pats. It was Hogie, my friend to the end. It seemed that he was always there when I desperately needed kindness and understanding.

Driving back to the Home after the Court of Honors, I sat in front with Hogie. What he said to our group was that he was proud of all of us. He said he was lucky to be able to work with boys as fine as us. His words served to end the evening on a happy note.

There was an important lesson for me, from that event. What I learned was that it's okay to try new things, and to over reach, even if you fail. And I learned that we need to be compassionate toward those who might fail. I fell asleep that night, wishing I could grow up to be like Hogie.

THE TREASURE OF CHARTER OAK

MRS. BABCOCK'S WILD RIDE

One of the funniest incidents that happened at the Home involved Mrs. Babcock, housemother of the girls, and my brother Earl.

Earl had left the Home in 1930, but a couple of years later, because there was no work to be found, he returned to the Home as an employee. His job was to work on the farm, and he also assumed an adult role in the dining room, sitting with the children, like the houseparents and other helpers.

Earl lived in the Help's Cottage now, just as a few other alumni were allowed to do once in a while.

One day, Mrs. Babcock asked Earl to teach her to drive. Not many women drove in those days, so it was a brave thing that she was attempting to do. She had a big, heavy car but didn't know how to drive it.

Earl agreed to teach her, and whenever he could get free from his farm duties, would take her out, trying to teach her the rudiments of managing the big machine.

One day we were all playing on the ball field, when we watched in horror as Mrs. Babcock at the wheel, and Earl looking frozen beside her, came barreling down toward the group of garages that stood on a sort of crest. Without slowing down, she made for the garage that had its door open; but instead of stopping, she continued right on, smashing through the backside of the garage. Goodby Mrs. Babcock and Earl! They disappeared over the crest and down the hill. A couple of us ran to the scene of the final stopping place of the car. Both Mrs. Babcock and Earl sat glued to their seats, unhurt, but very, very bowed!

BIG BROTHER WALTER—MY IDOL

Even though I was not raised with Walter, I admired this brother, who was ten years older than I. I tried to emulate whatever he did; I tried to do things that would impress him.

Because Walter had run the hurdles while in high school, I practiced running the hurdles at the Home, from the time I was nine or ten. I got ahold of some orange crates, set them yards apart, and then hurdled over the crates, using the proper style that I had watched at track meets. I hoped that I could eventually break school and league records, just as Walter had.

Imagine my excitement when Walter told me he had tickets to the Los Angeles Olympics, in 1932. No, not for track and field! Those cost money, and Walter was going to college on a shoestring. But the rowing events that were being held in Long Beach were free. And I got to go with Walter to see the finals of the eight-man rowing event.

We yelled and jumped up and down, as the rowboats came flying to the finish in the marina; the Golden Bears of University of California nosed out the Germans. And we hugged each other over the American victory.

I was only eleven years old, but that moment shared with my big brother was sweet. When he returned me to the Home, I felt ten feet tall, telling the boys in our dorm about the race. I wonder if Walt knew how much that day meant to me.

EARTHQUAKES AND CREAM PUFFS

It was the early part of 1933, while we were sitting in the dining room finishing dinner and looking forward to a once-in-a-lifetime dessert of cream puffs, when the walls began to tremble along with a horrible roaring sound.

"EARTHQUAKE! EARTHQUAKE!" screamed Mrs. Babcock, one of the housemothers. And she got up and streaked across the dining room to the double doors that led outside.

I was sorely tempted to remain behind to mind the cream puffs sitting at each place on the tables, but was swept up in the rush to get outside. Fortunately, Mrs. Pope, the dining room lady, kept her cool and made us slow down and file outside in pairs, keeping us from trampling each other. Mrs. Pope had experienced many earthquakes while living in Japan, and knew just what to do.

"Go out to the ball field, away from the buildings," she calmly ordered. And we obeyed...all except one culprit, it seemed.

We never did get to taste those cream puffs, because once assembled outside, we were not to return to the dining room. Instead, we were allowed to go quickly into our quarters, select two possessions, and then quickly return outside. We boys would spend the night in the Boy Scout house.

I gathered up the New Testament that had been given to me at the Shriners' Home, and also a framed photograph of my mother. Then I scurried out of the building to join the others on the edge of the baseball field, next to the first forest.

Fortunately, there were no further quakes, and we were able to return to our sturdy brick buildings the next morning. As important to us as the quake, was the question of what happened to those cream puffs. Someone said Mrs. Wade, the pantry lady, had gathered them up for the help to enjoy while we were at school.

But one of the guys had a different theory: "Hey, did you notice the cream on Butch's mouth, at the scout house?" Butch was not about to admit or deny it; after all, how many cream puffs could one boy eat? All we could do was fantasize about the delectable dessert we'd almost eaten. What an inopportune time for an earthquake!

MY PAL REMO

Although Remo and I played with all the other boys in our age group, inevitably we would spend more time together.

I was his good-luck charm whenever he played marbles; he would have me stand right behind him, while he wiped out everybody in pot, chase, and follow the course. The latter was a marble game we devised, with a course similar to a miniature golf course. No matter what the game, Remo would win, and was hailed as the Home's Miggs Champion.

One of the craziest schemes we shared was at Mrs. Pope's annual hot dog and soda pop picnic. The guys in our junior building started complaining about the dining room lady's annual effort, so Remo and I decided we'd spice it up. We decided we'd participate in a mock wedding, and it turned out that the wedding was the event of the year.

I tried to convince Remo to be the bride, but he refused to, so I was it. Some of the senior girls fashioned a skirt and veil for me, and Remo wore adult trousers and jacket; and in front of the administration building, with all the Home kids and help assembled in the driveway, Mr. Downen performed the mock ceremony. Pictures were taken of this great event, and Mrs. Pope's annual picnic took on a special meaning.

Rice was thrown, and everyone, howling with laughter, shouted, "Kiss the bride!" Remo blushed and refused, so to bring things to an end, I gave him a peck on the cheek.

It was a long time before everyone stopped referring to us as the bride and groom!

Another joint effort of ours didn't turn out so well. Our second summer at Bal, Remo and I discovered that Clemmo was snitching soda pop from Walley's Grocery Store on the Big Island. He was hiding it under his bed and then handing it out to different guys at night.

That's where Rem and I got the idea to go over and case Walley's; we didn't plan on stealing anything to start. But once we got there, Remo and I thought we might like some cookies. Of course, we had no money, so that meant we would have to steal the cookies.

"I can't steal," said Remo, "because my grandmother wouldn't like it." I presumed that Rem's grandmother was no longer living, but I could see that he had promised her at some time or another that he'd never steal.

"Okay," I said, "then I'll do it." It was the first time that I had even thought of stealing anything.

I went in and soon came out again with the box of illegal cookies. The two of us feasted on the goodies and threw away the box before returning to our barracks.

That night, a meeting was called, and Mr. Jones, our housefather, told us he knew about the stolen pop. He said everyone in the barracks would be severely punished if the guilty party did not confess.

Being a novice at this sort of thing, my conscience got the better of me. "I didn't steal the pop, but I did take some cookies from Walley's today," I confessed.

I didn't feel much like a hero when I got a paddling from Mr. Jones, right in front of the other boys. But I learned that stealing doesn't pay; not when you have a conscience.

Much later, in the sixth grade, Remo and I would come close to a falling out, one that nearly wrecked our friendship.

An election was held in class to choose the lead in a play, and the kids chose me. I felt pretty good about that, because I was somewhat of a ham and loved drama.

At the next recess, Remo said to me: "You're not going to

take that sissy part, are you?"

"It's not a sissy part, Rem."

"Well," replied Remo,"I sure wouldn't want the part!"

With that, I went to Miss Dust and told her that I didn't want to play the lead. She accepted my decision without a fuss, and I thought the matter was closed.

The next day, when Miss Dust began assembling the cast for a rehearsal, she announced that Remo would be playing the lead instead of Ivan. I nearly fainted!

The first chance I got, I confronted Remo with an irate, "How come? I thought that was a sissy part!"

Remo answered innocently: "Well, gosh, she asked me to take the part."

For a few days I was distant in my dealings with my best friend. But then, we just naturally drifted back together. We both figured it was more important to keep our friendship than to feud over a silly play.

We were true pals: he taught me to count in Italian, and I taught him to swim. I was his good luck charm at marble contests; he always backed me up when I had to fight more than one guy. It was a friendship that would last a lifetime!

Jackie McKinnon

TURNOVERS AND TURMOIL

In a time of unemployment in the outside world, it seemed incongruous that the houseparents in charge of us couldn't handle their job. Perhaps because of constant growth in numbers and crowded quarters, we boys in the Intermediate Dorm were hard to manage. But, in retrospect, it seems that Mr. Downen could have hired people who understood adolescence; there were plenty of former teachers out of work.

Each new housefather seemed worse than the last. When Mr. Jones left, he was replaced with Mr. Levine—a man who seldom smiled, and ultimately was as severe as Mr. Jones.

One day, Clemmo did a very serious thing; he pulled the rug that Mr. Levine was standing on right out from under him. Being kids, some of us snickered when the man fell. This enraged Mr. Levine so that he hauled off and smacked Eddie as hard as he could; he must have thought that Eddie caused him to fall. We just stood aghast, our mouths open at the sound of the blow; a welt formed on Eddie's face right before our eyes.

Bugs, who never got into trouble, stepped forward and took charge. Without saying a word to Mr. Levine, he took Eddie by the arm and led him to Mr. Downen's office. When the superintendent heard what had happened, he fired Mr. Levine.

Before we had time to heave a sigh of relief, the new housefather arrived. It was Bodie—the man who had witnessed my paddling by Mr. Jones. We didn't know it then, but we were in for far greater troubles than we had ever experienced before.

Bodie was not outwardly mean, at first. He did make sure that we saw the loaded German luger that he kept under his pillow; and he made it clear, in measured tones, that we would be expected to do everything he ordered.

Clemmo was kicked out of the Home, which did not surprise us. As naughty as we could be, we knew he had done a very dangerous thing to Mr. Levine.

But poor, sad Franzo was also banished. First, he was sent to live in the hospital because he was said to have a bad heart. But he was sent back to Bodie, and then in no time at all was sent away, this time to a reform school in Whittier. His sin? Franzo got poor grades at school, and he showed no interest in any of the activities in the Home.

Bodie started out by being extra nice to us boys. He'd make peanut butter fudge and treat us; he would take a few boys to the Covina Theater as a reward for being good; sometimes he'd invite us into his living quarters and tell us about his adventures when he was a soldier in Kaiser Wilhelm's army.

But we soon learned why he was being nice; one by one, he was approaching the boys, touching them, fondling them. It happened to me when he insisted that I sit on his lap on the way to Balboa. When we got back from Bal, we boys secretly met, and decided that Bodie's advances could no longer be tolerated. I offered to go to Mr. Downen.

I needn't have bothered! When I told Mr. Downen that Bodie was touching boys in their private parts, he exploded at me: "Never speak that way about a houseparent again!" He ordered me out of his office.

After that, Bodie became cold and stern toward us; as we resisted his advances, he became very angry. Privileges were revoked; punishment was swift for the slightest offense. He seemed highly nervous, and everything seemed to set him off.

One day, I moved my bed slightly, causing a smear in the polished hardwood floor. My punishment? A bloodied nose from Bodie's fist.

Things were getting out of hand, and we didn't know where to turn. Finally, in desperation, Remo told his older brother, Elbe, about our plight; Elbe instructed us to go on strike by refusing to go back into the dorm after supper.

Bodie kept clanging his hand bell, but we stood our ground. Soon, the clanging stopped, and as darkness fell,

Elbe told us to go inside. Bodie was not there; we were without adult supervision for the night. Someone found peanut butter fudge in Bodie's quarters and we had a feast.

We don't know to this day what transpired in the office of the superintendent; but someone had finally convinced Mr. Downen that Bodie had no business being with a bunch of young boys.

Bodie spent the night in the farm manager's cottage that night. The next morning, we saw Mr. Hess driving Bodie away in his truck—to where, we didn't know.

DEATH PAYS A VISIT

It was an odd thing that, even though almost all of us in the Home were there because of death in the family, we didn't discuss death. Once in a while a boy would be off alone crying because news had come that his parent had died. But the concept of death was not one that we understood.

So when it actually occurred at the Home, first the death of an animal, then the death of a person, it was a great shock.

Although we were not allowed to have pets (excepting Remo's pigeon Charley who mysteriously laid eggs), there was an old dog we called Togo. Although Togo belonged to the Moorheads across Badillo Street, he spent most of his time hanging around the Home.

Togo loved to watch us play Prisoner's Base, marbles, and softball...whatever activity was going on. We just took him for granted.

One day, as I was heading toward the farm, I met Russell, a kind senior boy, wheeling a wheelbarrow up the incline, heading toward the buildings. I stopped to look, and it was our adopted dog...he was dead.

"What happened?" I asked. Russell hemmed and hawed, then replied, "Well, he died of old age. Mr. Heard told me to take him across to the Moorheads and bury him."

Having petted and talked to Togo for so many years, I became very upset. I asked Russell if I could go with him, and he nodded "Yes."

While Russell held on to the wheelbarrow, I ran to the back porch of the old farm house and knocked on the screen door. Both Mr. and Mrs. Moorhead came out, and I could see how terrible this elderly couple felt when they saw their dear dog.

We offered to dig a grave for Togo; they pointed out a spot under a peach tree nearby. While we were digging, I stepped on a bee with my bare foot, and the pain was excruciating. I didn't say anything because I figured the poor couple had enough grief on their hands. I just rubbed the sole of my foot, and tried to keep back the tears...tears for the pain of losing that dog, as well as from the bee sting.

When we were finished, Mrs. Moorhead asked if she could give something for our help; we said "No," but finally accepted a peach off the tree.

Crossing Badillo back to the Home, my heart was heavy. Just the day before, I had played with Togo, talked to him, caressed his coat; and now he was lying in the ground. I'm glad that Russell didn't tell me what I later found out: that Mr. Heard, the carpenter, had poisoned the dog.

A second tragedy followed soon after we lost Togo. This time, it dealt with a human being: Mr. Hess, the farm manager.

Jackie was the one who discovered his body, gored by the bull. Jackie had spied two shiny black boots sticking out from under the fence, and leaning down to examine them, he realized they were on Mr. Hess. He looked over the fence and saw that the man was lying still. Running like mad toward Mr. Downen's office, he stopped long enough to ask Goofy for his shirt so that he wouldn't have to see the superintendent without being properly clad.

A group of boys gathered around the fence, waiting for help to come. Finally, a doctor arrived and gave a shot to

Mr. Hess's heart, but it was too late. Mr. Hess was dead.

It was announced that anyone wishing to could attend Mr. Hess's Funeral. Quite a number of us went. We sat ever so quietly in the mortuary chapel as the service was begun. It was terribly sad to bid good-by to this adult who had always been so kind to us.

And we weren't the only ones feeling this loss. Sitting nearby, with tears streaming down her pretty face, was the young woman who was to have married Mr. Hess in a few weeks.

I found myself watching her and identifying with her. Someone close had been taken away, altering the course of her life.

Death had invaded the Home twice within a few weeks; death with its eeriness and mystery. We were driven back to the Home after the funeral; not one word was spoken. Each of us, in his own way, was trying to understand how life could be so precarious and impermanent.

OFF TO SMITTY'S GRANDMA'S HOUSE

It was strange that most of us remembered one or both parents at some point in our lives, but seldom did anyone mention grandparents. I don't think I had ever met a grandparent.

So it was a real adventure one Sunday when Smitty mentioned he'd like to hike to Pomona, not telling us that that was where his grandmother lived.

Hiking was one of the joys of our life. There was a certain kind of freedom involved; so Smitty didn't have to coax us. Franzo had again returned to the Home, so he said, "Yeah, let's go!" Ed and I were eager to join in, too, so without giving it a thought, we planned on the hike to Pomona, which lay twelve miles away.

We left right after finishing the breakfast dishes from the weekly pancake treat. We figured we could make it there and back by supper time.

Instead of following Garvey Boulevard east, we struck out into the hills, running up and down with abandon. By noon, we arrived in Pomono, breathless and thirsty. And it was then that Smitty sprung his surprise: "Hey, guys, my grandma lives near here; let's go see her!"

We walked the few blocks to his grandmother's house, and stood there looking at the neat wood frame, surrounded by a picket fence. With flowering shrubs in front, it looked like a story-book house.

By the time we had reached the front door, Grandma had come out on the front porch. She hugged Smitty and then invited us in.

Inside, the house smelled of spices and sugar. The place was neat, though small and overfilled with heavy furniture. I felt warm and comfortable. Funny, I can't remember what she gave us for lunch, but I do know that in a while she served us baked apple for dessert.

Baked apple? I'd never tasted it before, but it was so delicious. In the Home, dessert was usually canned fruit cocktail or pudding (except for homemade ice cream on Sundays).

So this is how it is in a normal home, I thought to myself. Other kids had parents and grandparents who lived in warm and cozy houses surrounded by picket fences. Why couldn't my mother live in a place like this?

I knew that Smitty's mother had died, leaving three small children behind. Their father, an oil field worker, knew that he could not stay at home with his kids, and so had placed them in the Home.

"Why," I wondered, "hadn't this nice grandmother taken in the children?" I guess Mr. Smith, being a Mason and knowing about the Home, had felt that that was the place for his young ones. And maybe Grandma wasn't up to taking care of young kids at her age.

But I just loved being there in that house with that sweet, plump lady, just for that little while. Something inside me stirred, a yearning that I could not have been able to put into words. I guess I was mourning the absence of something I never had.

On the hike back to the Home, each of us was very quiet. My thoughts were again about why my mother couldn't have kept me, her baby, with her. Some parents who had put their older children into the Home held onto their babies. I wondered why that couldn't have been my case.

But I knew the answer: my mother had not been able to cope with the responsibility of even one of her children. Even as a baby, I had been placed with a lady who nursed me when I had small pox—a disease that killed quite a few people in the early twenties.

Mother did what she had to do; and I had to again admit to myself that my being placed in the Home was for the better. At least I lived in clean surroundings and had good friends like Franzo, Ed and Smitty.

We reached the Home just as the supper siren was blowing. Tired as we were, we ran to the dining room and stood behind our chairs just in time for the blessing. We ate our light supper of cinnamon and rice with milk, not caring that we had missed the good Sunday dinner followed by ice cream. It was worth it. We'd been to Grandmother's house!

A LAUREL AND HARDY TRICK BACKFIRES

There were only three boys I knew of who came to the Home from states other than California; one from Utah, one from Oregon, and Benny from Arizona. The first two were much older than myself, and I didn't really know them well. Benny was my age and in my class, and we became close pals.

Benny was a mellow kid at peace with himself and others. We enjoyed working around the farm together, he sloshing around in oversized milk boots and wearing an old derby hat.

It was during the eighth grade that Benny and a few other boys were down near the farm playing Pee Wee, a game we'd seen in a Laurel and Hardy comedy. It was played by hitting a small, oval piece of wood with a stick and making the piece fly up in the air.

Pee Wee, like so many other free-time activities, was potentially dangerous, but no one told us we couldn't play. We assumed it was okay.

This particular day, Benny was standing too close to the boy in front of him who had the stick, and when the stick was swung, it accidentally hit Benny in the eye.

Benny was blinded in the one eye and had to be fitted with a glass eye. He seemed to get along pretty well, and in spite of days of absences caused by the accident, he graduated with us from Charter Oak and was looking forward to attending Covina High School in the fall.

But that was not to be. During the summer, Benny's

other eye began to redden, and his vision began to blur. He checked himself into the Home hospital, where it was thought that the chlorine from the newly built swimming pool was causing the problem. In reality, the functioning eye had become infected, and before summer's end, Benny's eyesight had failed altogether.

Before Benny left to attend the State School for the Blind in Berkeley, he asked me to walk him down to the farm one last time. When we got to the shed, he told me that he wanted me to have his milk boots and old derby hat. "Think of me when you wear these, and when you're working here on the farm," he said. I promised him I would.

It was sad to say goodby to this fine boy. Because of one careless moment, his whole life was changed.

Each summer, Benny would come to visit us at the Home. At the institute for the blind, he had not only learned to read braille, but he had become a very good guitarist. I remember looking over at the adults one evening when he was playing for us, and there were tears in the adults' eyes.

Benny remained as serene and accepting of his lot as he had been before the accident. He would not have wanted anyone to cry for him.

(The last time I saw Benny was at an Alumni Reunion at the Home in 1949. He was married to a nice lady who was also blind.)

ADULT KINDNESS REJECTED

I craved attention and kindness, and probably love as well; yet when it was extended to me, I didn't know how to handle it.

I was beginning to build a wall around my emotions, in an effort to act tough when confronted with rejection and punishment. I was crusty on the outside of a very fragile inside. I was beginning to accept the fact that I would not be receiving love in the Home.

So when Mrs. Russum, our new housefather's wife, showed an interest in me and tried to show that she cared about my inner feelings, I felt very uncomfortable.

She was really a nice lady. For three Fridays in a row she arranged to take me to the Covina Theater, along with the senior boys and girls. She sat with me and chatted with me in the theater, and after the show, riding back in the bus.

When she asked me on the fourth Friday, I told her I didn't want to go anymore. She asked me why, and I told her that some of the boys in my dorm were teasing me and giving me a bad time. What I didn't tell her, and couldn't express, was that I just couldn't handle her kindness. I recognized the fact that she knew I had a deep need for adult attention, and that embarrassed me. She could see through my toughness? Well, I couldn't have that. If I lowered my defenses, I would be hurt. So, instead of taking that chance, I rejected this kind lady's attempt to help me relax and trust adults.

When Friday came, I told myself that I was glad that I didn't have to go to the Covina Theater that night. But I already felt the void that I had deliberately created.

SENIOR BOYS' BUILDING

I was the first of our gang to move from the Intermediate Dorm to the Senior Building. I guess it was because my housefather, Mr. Russum, considered me a kind of rowdy.

One evening, after he caught four of us boys having an orange fight down in the basement, Mr. Russum marched us up to our quarters and then, one by one, called us into his office to receive punishment for our poor behavior. As each boy came out, I asked what happened, and the reply was that the oranges had to be cleaned up and the floor washed down. Mr. Russum didn't believe in corporal punishment, and I really did like him.

He saved me for last. As soon as I sat down across from him, he said, "Ivan, I'm not going to punish you. But I'm going to ask you a question, and I want an honest answer. Do you like me?"

There it was again! Kindness was being shown me. But instead of telling him that I thought he was a good housefather, I answered, "No."

"That's all I wanted to know", Mr. Russum said, and then he told me that there was one opening in the Senior building and I would be sent there.

I guessed that his reasons were that he thought I had been the ring leader in the orange fight mess, and that moving in with older boys would help tone me down. But it didn't matter. I was happy that I would be going to the Senior building.

There were more privileges there. Boys could stay up till 10:00 p.m. instead of 9:00 p.m.; I would be eating in the big kids' dining room; and I would be able to earn money working at the Home, after school and on weekends.

I moved into my room upstairs and settled in. There were three beds to a room now; I felt very grown up. Mr. and Mrs. Bedord, my new houseparents, seemed all right; I vowed to stay out of their way.

I soon found out that, along with privileges, there would be added responsibilities. From here on, I would be expected to pay for my own school clothes and shoes. I would also need to buy my own toilet articles such as soap, toothpaste, toothbrush, and combs.

Whereas the boys and girls in the junior buildings had not worked for pay, senior residents could earn money for specific jobs. During the school year I would be able to earn two cents under my age. (At age 13 I would receive eleven cents an hour.) But during summers the rate of pay was ten cents under my age, meaning a rate of three cents an hour. The lower rate of pay for summer was meant to offset the fact that one could work so many more hours than during the regular school year.

Just as junior boys had been expected to take care of their rooms, sweep the walks, polish floors, and do dining room work without pay, senior building residents were also expected to do so. Paying jobs were those like helping in the laundry, working on the farm, doing pots and pans, and cleaning the Downens' cottage.

Senior girls had paying jobs in the office and in the hospital, taking trays to patients, doing first aid, and answering the phone.

For us, Mr. Bedord kept strict accounts of hours worked, money earned, and money spent. It was a good learning experience for us.

While in the Intermediate Dorm, I had put claim to a crystal set that one of the older boys had left behind. I had loved putting the earphones on at night and listening to the squeaky, squawky music and voices. It was great because I had been able to relax and enjoy myself without disturbing anyone. Reluctantly, I had left the crystal set when I moved to the Senior building.

But I was really lucky when, soon after settling in, a friend of my mother's brought me a table radio. This became my prized possession, which I proudly shared with the older guys.

Each evening, they'd gather in my room to listen to such programs as "One Man's Family," "Calling All Cars," "The Green Hornet," "Mandrake the Magician," "Jack Benny," and "The Eddie Cantor Show." My favorite program was "Jack Armstrong, All American Boy."

Squeaking doors, eerie moans, and weird voices kept us riveted to the radio as we listened with lights out. Our imaginations took over as we hung on to every scary word.

Another thing I enjoyed listening to were the fights which were broadcast from either the American Legion Hall or the Olympic Auditorium. It was amazing how the announcers were able to describe every blow and movement of each boxer. Often, I'd find myself emulating the fighters by jabbing, weaving, and delivering uppercuts during the broadcast. Listening to the radio was one of the pleasures I will always associate with my life in the senior building.

GOODBY CHARTER OAK...HELLO, COVINA HIGH

I especially enjoyed my last two years at Charter Oak Grammar School. I liked having male teachers—Mr. Boots in seventh grade, and Mr. Reynolds, who was the principal as well as the eighth grade teacher.

It wasn't that I disliked any of my women teachers. Miss Cooper in the fifth grade was pretty and sweet; I think all of us boys had a secret crush on her. And Miss Dust, our sixth grade teacher, was strict, demanding, and very professional, winning our respect. I remember her full name because she wrote songs, and when we were giving a program, whoever announced the song had to say, "By Laurel M. Dust."

But the men teachers were different. They got out on the ball field with us; they shot baskets with us, and often played on our basketball teams. I can't remember ever getting into trouble with either "Boots" or Mr. Reynolds. They knew how to channel young boys' energies. They encouraged us to use our competitiveness, with an awareness of fair play and good sportsmanship. They arranged track meets and basketball games with surrounding grammar schools like San Dimas and Laverne.

After a sporting event, I would often purposely miss the school bus home so that I could talk with "Boots" or Mr. Reynolds. And then I'd walk back to the Home, cutting through the orange groves, chasing quail, and always stopping to check an oak tree or two, to see if I could spot the hidden charter.

On the final leg of the trip to the Home, I'd daydream about what I'd do with all the treasure if I ever found out where it was hidden. Then suddenly I'd snap back to reality, and would run the rest of the way home. I'd fairly fly upstairs to my room, just in time to change into dungarees, and head for the farm for an hour's work before supper.

In June, 1935, just before my fourteenth birthday, we graduated from Charter Oak. I hated leaving my favorite teachers behind, but looked forward to a more grown-up world in high school.

Covina High School was situated right in the heart of town, on Citrus Avenue. The population of the town in the fall of 1935 was 1,999. The reason I know that is that one day, when Eddie Lord and I were walking downtown, a photographer took our picture which eventually ended up on a postcard showing the downtown section; and it had on it: "Population, 1,999." Eddie and I picked up a bunch of the cards from Tucker's Studio and distributed them to our pals.

Up to the time I went to high school, I hadn't had much to do with Covina. I'd had my tonsils out in the hospital there, and had gone to the movies a few times; but I hadn't really identified with this typical American town.

Actually, Covina was famous throughout the United States because it was the location in the Harold Teen comic strip. All the places mentioned in the funnies were real. There actually was a Pop who ran the Sugar Bowl; and the

Covina National Bank and Covina Theater, as well as the Argus Newspaper, really existed.

Each year, at Covina High, students voted for a Harold Teen and his girlfriend Lillums to reign at a special school dance.

So it was that, although few people knew about our Home nestled in the groves near Charter Oak, Americans everywhere were reading about Covina in the Sunday and daily papers.

I looked forward to becoming a Covina Colt and participating in school sports for the next four years. I planned to play football and run track for Coach Pendleton.

As soon as school opened in the fall, I turned out for football. As a freshman and still very light in weight, I played on the B team, as a quarterback. Our team wasn't very good, but that didn't really matter. Home Kids and Outsiders enjoyed playing football together.

In future years, I would gain a lot of height and would fill out some, and so would play on the line as tackle. It was a lot more fun at that position, since I wouldn't have to feel stressed out trying to remember signals and calling plays.

Track and field turned out to be my favorite sport, though. It was something I could do individually, taking responsibility for my own performance. Besides broad jumping (now it's called the long jump), I ran dashes and the 120 low hurdles. Coach Pendleton was amazed at my ability to hurdle so naturally; I told him how I had been inspired by my big brother, and how I had been jumping over makeshift hurdles for years...first orange crates, then wooden hurdles I'd made in the Charter Oak woodshop class.

What a thrill it was when I made my letter in track in my freshman year. In addition, I was selected to run in the CIF (California Interscholastic Federation) finals in Whittier.

That same season, I got to participate in the Carpinteria Relays, which was an invitational meet. Our high school team got to stay overnight in Carpinteria; we had rooms in a motel situated right along Highway 101.

Three to a room, each group was responsible for

shopping for food, cooking meals, and cleaning up. That was a piece of cake for those who had come from the Home. It was a lot of fun, and though I didn't know it at the time, I would be doing this again in my sophomore and junior years.

It was interesting talking with the two Outsiders who shared my room; their perspective about school and their future was different from mine. They seemed to be very secure about their plans, whereas I wasn't sure how I would attain my goals. I did share with my roommates my desire to become a coach some day. I thought Coach Pendleton had the greatest of all jobs, working with youth, encouraging them, and molding their skills and their character.

As usual, I couldn't sleep. My mind was filled with the excitement of the day's track meet, and the dreams I had shared with my friends. Outside the window, cars and trucks whizzed by; I counted the whizzes, wishing that I could fall asleep.

Ivan

COACH REYNOLDS—AGE 15

My wish to become a coach came true sooner than I had envisioned. Of course, it wasn't as a college graduate like Oak Pendleton, but I did become a coach.

At the Home, we had formed a basketball team, which was a continuation from our days at Charter Oak. All five of us turned out for basketball at Covina High. When Coach Pendleton selected only Junior and me for the Colt team, I rebelled. I told him, in a cocky manner, that if our whole Home team couldn't play, then Junior and I wouldn't play for him.

Now a kid had no business telling the coach who should and shouldn't be selected for the high school basketball team. But I was all charged up, and said to our guys, "Let's challenge Covina High's team!" The Home boys agreed with enthusiasm.

With no adult interested in coaching us, the task fell naturally to me. The five of us practiced fiercely, in anticipation of playing the Colts. When we were confident enough, I went to Coach Pendleton and told him that the Home boys would like to play his Colts. Oak readily agreed.

At game time, the crowd in the high school gym was drawn into two distinct groups: the Home kids and the Outsiders. Each side wildly cheered when the two teams came onto the floor. We warmed up, passing and shooting for a few minutes, and then the contest began.

Victory came easy to us; because the five of us had lived with each other for so many years, our reflexes were sharper than those of our opponents. We knew each other's moves automatically.

Basking with that win, and with our enthusiastic Home fans behind us, we felt like taking on all comers. With Mr. Bedord's permission, I used the office phone to call surrounding schools to set up a schedule. I told the heads of those teams that I was the coach, not revealing the fact that I was only fifteen. I was afraid that if they knew, they wouldn't take me seriously.

The schedule had us playing each team twice; we were to play Cal Prep, Citrus High, Sherman Institute for Indians, The Voorhis School for Boys, and Chino Boys' Republic. In addition, Coach Pendleton agreed to play us again.

Since the Home had no basketball court, our team did its practicing at Charter Oak Grammar School. As basketball fever grew to a pitch among the Home kids, Mr. Bedord acknowledged the importance of all this and agreed to let us buy uniforms. These were plain white tops and shorts. We didn't indulge ourselves with sweat clothes as that would have been too expensive.

Since all the games were played away, our Home bus would load on the kids and transport them to and from each game. It was great hearing my sister Julie and her friends cheering us on, and to hear Helen and Verna, my good friends and classmates, yelling, "Come on, Home Boys!" With that kind of support, we got through the whole schedule undefeated!

I took my role as a coach very seriously, even sending for professional literature and products through the mail. One time I sent for a sample of Postum, signing the order with Coach Ivan Reynolds, and they sent a whole case of free Postum. Each night we'd pour hot water from the tap over the stuff and indulge ourselves. I decided that being a coach was fulfilling in more ways than one!

FRANZO

Every Sunday night before bedtime, everyone was required to write to a relative, if they had one. Whether or not we received a letter in return depended on what our individual circumstances were. Once in a while I would receive a letter from Mother, and that gave me incentive to write the next letter.

Now, when Franzo had first come to the Home, we all thought he was an orphan; but then he told us he had a mother in Northern California, so he joined the rest of us in writing the Sunday night letters.

One day, when I was reading one of my mother's letters, I noticed that Franzo seemed upset.

"What's wrong, Franz?" I asked.

"How come I never hear from my mother?" he responded.

"Well," I said, "you write to her every week, so you know she's alive. Why don't we go and ask Mr. Downen about it?"

When Franzo agreed, we started out together to confront Mr. Downen with the question. When we entered his office, Franzo asked the superintendent why there were never any letters from his mother, despite the fact that he wrote her every week.

His reply was: "Your mother doesn't know anyone. She's in a mental hospital in Stockton. She's been there ever since your father was killed. Even if you should visit her, she wouldn't know you."

Franzo and I were stunned by his answer.

"Then why did I write to her all this time? Why didn't you tell me about this, Mr. Downen?"

"Because I didn't think you could handle the truth," he replied.

With that, we walked out into a world that had just collapsed around my friend. He asked me if that meant his mother was insane. I nodded, and tried to comfort him, but he was not to be comforted. He felt deceived, and he was angry. For the next few days, he wandered around in a daze.

From that time on, Franzo lost all interest. He no longer cared about entering into adventurous schemes, and his schoolwork, which had begun to improve, slid back to what it had been before.

Franzo was excused from writing any more letters. When we sat writing our letters, he just sat and stared out at nothing. I really felt bad that I had been the one to encourage him to go to Mr. Downen. I told him I was sorry, but he didn't care about apologies.

The Home, having tried everything they knew to deal with the situation, decided to send Franzo away again, this time to a so-called uncle. The man was not actually related, but had been a friend of the family. That didn't last long; Franzo ran away and came back to the Home.

Mr. Downen let Franzo back into the Home, assigning him to the senior building. But that lasted only a few months. Franzo ran away, and this time ended up on skid row in L.A.

Mr. Schiff, our engineer, found him there—dirty with matted hair—and brought him back to stay with him in the Help's Cottage.

The next time he ran away, no one went after him. I wasn't to see Franzo again until the war, when he joined the Marines and served in the Pacific. He was in on the invasion of Saipan and Tarawa, where he fought bravely and with distinction.

THE MISSING 75 CENTS

I was concentrating on making my stay in the senior building smooth without running into trouble with Mr. or Mrs. Bedord. I had a feeling that Mrs. Bedord didn't especially like me, and I tried even harder to stay out of her way. Looking back, I don't think she cared too much for any of us.

Mr. Bedord would get on my case for not having better grades, but that was about all. He would post everyone's grades on the bulletin board for all to see. It seemed like the same guys always made the A's and B's. My best grades were in sports, art, and math. That meant that I spent each evening down in the basement studying, along with quite a few others.

But hard as I tried, trouble seemed to find me. Joe, one of my roommates, was given 75 cents by his dad one Sunday on visiting day. The next day, after school, Joe and I walked to the Sugar Bowl and he treated me to a root beer float. We both enjoyed sitting in Pop's malt shop, sipping our treats.

When we got back to the Home, Goofy, our other roommate said, "Hey, you guys are really in trouble with Mr. Bedord."

"What for?" we asked.

"Well, 75 cents has been stolen from some kid, and you two were reported having something at the Sugar Bowl after school."

We went right over to Mr. Bedord to let him know that Joe had gotten the money from his dad the day before. Mr. Bedord wouldn't let us explain; he just kept accusing us of stealing the money. For punishment, he said all privileges would be taken away for a month, and we would have to sit on chairs beside our beds, doing absolutely nothing for the next two days. The only time we could leave was to go to the dining room.

While he was chastising us, Joe began to turn pale and began to bend over with pain. This didn't deter Mr. Bedord.

He said it served Joe right for having the sweets at the Sugar Bowl. We left our housefather and went to our room to sit in our chairs.

When dinner time came, Joe said he couldn't go because of the pain on his right side. He just sat there doubled over.

I went to dinner and came back to my chair. By this time Joe was suffering so much that I had Goofy go to Mr. Bedord for help.

When Mr. Bedord saw Joe, he realized that this was something really serious. Joe was taken to the Covina Hospital that night where they removed his infected appendix.

After my two days of confinement were up, the kid who had reported his 75 cents missing found it. He had placed it in a secret place for safe keeping, and then had forgotten about it. Mr. Bedord told me that he was going to release me from further punishment.

I felt like telling him that all he had to do was check with Joe's dad; but that would have been pressing my luck.

There was never an apology to Joe or to me. That's just the way it was!

THE GREAT WAFFLE PARTY

Whenever the valley's temperature dipped below 32 degrees, everything focused on protecting the citrus crops. Even schools were closed, because the skies were black from smudging. Besides, closing the schools allowed the high school boys to help with the smudging.

One particular winter, the temperatures dipped below the 32-degree danger level and stayed in the low twenties for two weeks. I asked Mr. Bedord if I could help with the smudging, but he said no. I was very disappointed, because school was out, and it was a chance to earn the 35 cents an hour that the ranchers were paying the kids. Several of our senior building boys were given permission to light the pots during the night.

One Thursday, on Mr. Bedord's day off, Joe came home, exhausted from filling smudge pots, and asked me if I would take his place.

"Sure," I agreed, and for the next five days, I worked across the street in the groves where the Moorheads lived, filling the pots with oil, which would be heated later to keep the fruit from freezing.

Mr. Bedord knew I was working, so I assumed that Joe had told him the circumstances leading to my taking his place. When the rancher came to the Home to pay the kids who had helped, Mr. Bedord told him that I was not to be paid, because I had worked without his permission.

The rancher argued and argued with Mr. Bedord, telling him that I had been an especially reliable and hard worker. Without sounding disrespectful, I told Mr. Bedord that I had honestly assumed that it was okay for me to work, since he saw me leaving each day to go across the street, and he saw how sooty my clothes were upon my return.

"You didn't say anything to me, then," I said. "In fact, one day I even told you I was leaving to go help with the smudging."

Mr. Bedord was adamant. He insisted that I had disobeyed him, and he told the rancher that I would not be allowed to receive any pay.

Seeing that the matter had come to a standstill, the rancher gave Mr. Bedord the $30 that I had earned, and left. He figured he had done his part to do the right thing.

Mr. Bedord called the boys together and announced that we were going to have a waffle party with my earnings...and that was what took place. For my part, I refused to have anything to do with the party, and didn't eat a waffle.

I'd always been good in math, and I knew that forty waffles couldn't possibly cost $30; especially when the ingredients came out of the Home kitchen.

I couldn't help but wonder what Mr. Bedord really did with my hard-earned $30.

BUILDING FENCES AND DEFENSES

Through the years, because I was always getting myself into skirmishes and controversies, I became used to taking whatever punishment was meted out. I didn't intentionally get into trouble, and I never got into bad trouble. But I couldn't seem to please Mr. and Mrs. Bedord.

Because my grades weren't great, I was always down in the basement with the other guys who were in the same boat. The Bedords caused a labelling of kids, and a wedge between high achievers and low achievers in school.

Privileges like attending plays at the Pasadena Playhouse always went to the same guys. That was right, of course; but why didn't they offer that privilege to us for improving our grades? That would have given us some incentive to do better.

Anyway, I convinced myself that I didn't want to go anywhere in a group. Too often I had heard people whisper: "Oh, there go those poor orphans." The last time it had happened was when we'd gone to see some car races.

More and more, I became a loner. I spent more and more time working on the farm; and at school, my energies were put into sports.

I used reverse psychology on the Bedords, knowing that they would use denial of going somewhere as punishment. In my junior year, I even said I didn't want to go to the Monrovia Christmas Party. Mr. Bedord snapped back: "You have to go to the party." I figured I had him. At least he wouldn't threaten to leave me behind for the party. I'd built my fences around me, and they were helping me to cope.

IVAN—OUR TYPICAL HOME BOY

One evening, just after supper, Mr. Downen came over to me and said he'd like to speak with me. My stomach did a flip flop...what had I done now?

What he told me just about floored me. He told me that he had selected me to speak before the Monrovia Lodge members at their next meeting.

"They asked me to bring the most typical boy and girl to tell them about life in the Home. I think of you as being very typical. I think you can do a good job, especially since you have been here for ten years."

I didn't know it just then, but Dorothy Jordan was given the same invitation by Mr. Downen; we two were the ones honored.

On the evening of the lodge meeting, Dorothy and I rode with Mr. Downen to Monrovia. We felt at home here, since we came to the Christmas party year after year.

When Mr. Downen introduced me, he said I was just an average boy...with average grades in school, and average behavior in the Home. He told them what a hard worker I was on the farm, and how successful I was in sports.

My speech flowed easily. After all, I was relating my life in the Home as it happened day by day. I sat down, relieved at their enthusiastic applause, but then jumped up, clasping my head, and said, "Oh, no! I forgot to tell you about Christmas!" This brought about a roar from the assembled men...after all, they were the ones who gave us the fabulous party each year.

Dorothy did a good job telling about the girls' activities, and she, too, received a round of applause. Mr. Downen beamed with pride, as lodge members came up, one be one, congratulating him on doing such a fine job at the home.

They also praised Dorothy and me for our speeches, and thanked us for being a credit to the home.

One the way back, Mr. Downen talked to us animatedly. You could tell that he felt good about the evening, and the way Dorothy and I had presented ourselves.

I felt good about things as I got ready for bed that night. Next month, my junior year would be over, and I would be looking forward to a great senior year at Covina High.

There was nothing ominous in the air, nothing to warn me about events to come.

I fell asleep easily that night, smelling the sweet orange blossoms, and feeling on top of the world.

Mr. and Mrs. Downen

THE LAST SUMMER

I loved working on the farm. All of us in the senior building were required to work at least six hours a week, but my hours on the farm always exceeded the minimum.

Saturdays and summers gave me the opportunity to work long hours. Soon I had accumulated over $100, and became the only one to open an account at the Covina National Bank. By the time I would be leaving the Home, I would have earned $127—the fruit of working on the farm, sometimes for 70 hours a week.

During my freshman year, Jimmy Monroe and I worked together, under the supervision of the farm manager. There were hundreds of chickens to be fed, and their eggs had to be collected, sorted, and candled. In addition, fifty head of hogs needed to be fed, and the dairy cows had to be stripped after the milker had done the main part of the milking.

During my last two summers in the Home, I was the only kid working on the farm. I liked my job for the money, of course; but just as important, I enjoyed working outside. I didn't mind the sweltering valley heat, even when I was boiling potatoes for the pigs. The potatoes were sold to us for 30 cents per hundred pounds.

Always a skinny guy, I began to notice that muscles were forming on my arms, and I was able to lift heavy loads of hay. I was able to work right alongside the hay truck driver, lifting, carrying, and stacking the bales of hay.

Working summers meant that I had to give up going to Bal, but I truly didn't mind. Sometimes I'd ride over to Balboa with Mr. Bedord on a Saturday night, returning on Sunday.

One reason that I'd given up on going to Bal was because of what happened the summer after I completed my freshman year. I had gone over to the Big Island and found myself a job; but when I told Mr. Bedord about it, he told me I

84

couldn't work in Bal. He gave the job to Bob Riddell instead.

After that incident, I didn't care to stay in Bal. I told myself that I much preferred staying at the Home and working on the farm. I convinced myself that all that sand in my bed at night wasn't all that great...even if it meant that I'd miss out on swimming and surfing.

Actually, it was nice being at the Home with only a handful of kids and very few adults. This summer I got to help Joe's dad, who was hired to do the painting while the majority of the kids were at Balboa. I really liked working with this kind man.

One day, when I became ill from smelling paint, he gently led me to my room to lie down, and kept coming in to check on me. I figured Joe was a lucky guy to have a dad like that. In my estimation, he was right up there with the Blairs' dad who taught me to play chess, and Phil's dad who played checkers with me on his Sunday visits.

There was a hot plate down in the shed, where different guys had tried to cook squab or make fudge. One day I asked Mrs. Bedord if she had a fudge recipe, and she handed one to me. She told me to get the ingredients from the kitchen, so I thought it was okay to make fudge in the shed.

The fudge turned out pretty well. In fact, I was so proud of it that I went to Mrs. Bedord and offered her a piece. She took it without a word of thanks, but then started scolding me for having ripped my dungarees the day before. I explained that I was afraid I'd be late to dinner, had jumped a fence, and ripped the leg. I added that there hadn't been time to change.

I recalled that those pants had been missing the next morning, but didn't give it any further thought.

Well, instead of accepting my explanation, she sternly told me to accompany her to Mr. Downen's office. She brought along the torn pants, and the fudge, resting on a piece of toilet paper.

When she showed the evidence of my carelessness and willful breaking of rules, Mr. Downen suppressed a smile. I think the candy sitting on the piece of toilet paper struck him as funny. He didn't say much to me; but I noticed a silent kind of signal passing between him and Mrs. Bedord.

I didn't know it then, but this episode was a part of the case Mrs. Bedord was making to persuade Mr. Downen to consider the possibility of my going to live with my mother. Within a week of the fudge incident, I, who had just a month before been selected to speak before the Monrovia Lodge as a typical Home boy, would be notified that I would have to leave the Home.

When the news came, I was stunned! I knew that sometimes I had been stubborn and contrary; but I had never done anything mean or dangerous. My free spirit was a survival tool. Without it, I would have knuckled under.

There was no one to talk to; no one to console me. I decided then to take that hike up to Buzzard's Peak. And I took with me the pennant that I would plant in memory of the ten years I had spent in this place.

That hike was the consummation of my childhood, and the beginning of I knew not what.

THE TREASURE OF CHARTER OAK

EPILOGUE

As I put my things into Mrs. Knowles's car for the trip to my mother's, my main thought was that I wouldn't be able to say goodby to my friends. Since they were all at Balboa, they wouldn't even know I had to leave until their return at summer's end. I felt just terrible!

My only conversation with Mrs. Knowles was when I asked why I was being kicked out when I hadn't done anything bad. Her curt reply was: "You aren't being kicked out; you're just not wanted."

Add that hurt to the shock of having to leave my home of ten years, and you have the picture. I just sat quietly for the remainder of the drive to the house, which was on Menlo Street, right off Vermont. The University of Southern California was about a half mile from the house, which was, for the moment, being shared by Mother, Walter, his wife May, and Earl. From the verdant San Gabriel Valley to the heart of Los Angeles!

Mrs. Knowles had convinced Mr. Downen that the Reynolds family was all together, living in harmony; that was her rationalization for having dismissed me from the Home. She pulled up in front of the fourplex, waited until I unloaded my few belongings, and then drove off without a fare-thee-well, and apparently with a free conscience.

With a heavy heart, I picked up my box of belongings and went to the front door. When I rang the bell, Mother came to the door. She didn't look especially happy to see me; in fact, I detected a look of apprehension. Inside, I nodded to Walt, May, and Earl who also appeared uncomfortable with this new situation. My heart sank. Something told me that this new arrangement was not going to work.

My feelings proved to be correct. By the time the first week had passed, I realized that the atmosphere between the members of the family was heavy with discontent and anger.

87

I had barely put away my things in the living room which was to double as my bedroom, when I was told that I would have to contribute to the family budget. Instead of having the presence of mind to let them know that my $127 check would be arriving, I said I'd go out and look for a job.

Seeking a job turned out to be a fiasco. The stock reply from people who interviewed me was that family men were desperately seeking employment. They all asked me why I didn't return to school. Well, I couldn't let them know that I was being required to pay room and board.

I decided that I'd join the Navy. That way, the family wouldn't have to worry about me, and I wouldn't have to worry about finding a job. Mother agreed to sign for me, since I was under age, but that didn't work out, either. I failed the physical because of albumin in my urine. It is interesting to note that a few years later the Navy would take me happily, regardless of albumin.

What happened next was to affect the next ten years of my life. The family broke up: Walter and May went their way, and Earl and Mother moved to a small apartment. I felt like a straw blowing in the wind. Alone...all alone!

I drifted from one place to another. For a while I rode the freights up and down California, doing odd jobs here and there. I joined the Civilian Conservation Corps, and worked up in the Sequoia National Forest, helping to build a road to Independence. The project was eventually abandoned because of inpenetrable terrain; you can imagine the conditions. It was winter when I arrived, and the men in CCC lived in flimsy army barracks. We worked side by side with convicts from Folsom Prison. Fortunately, their living quarters were on the opposite side of the camp.

When the CCC stint was done, I returned to Southern California and found a job as night messenger with the Postal Telegraph Company in Long Beach. For a few months, I shared an apartment with Mother and my sister Julie. When Mother took off, without a word to us, that arrangement fell apart.

By now, my friends in the Masonic Home had graduated.

From time to time I would see them; most were either joining a service or were waiting to get in. For a short while, Smitty's dad took me in, when I had nowhere else to go.

Eventually, I ended up in Seattle, working as a carpenter's helper with a group of Norwegians. A short stint in the Merchant Marines also took place, before I went in the Navy after Pearl Harbor was bombed.

Remo was on the USS West Virginia when the attack came. He told me later that he thought about my teaching him to swim at Bal, when he was swimming to shore with bombs falling all around. As it turned out, Remo would participate in every major Pacific naval battle of World War II. He remained in the Navy for twenty years, and retired as Chief Gunner's Mate. A true hero, and certainly a credit to the Masonic Home!

So many Home boys gave their lives for their country during World War II. From my age group alone there were Jim Blair, Bob Countryman, Melvin Rouch, Ralph Peterson, Joe Wagnon, Fred Burgen, Walter Smith (Smitty's brother), and Clemmo. How sad that they never had a chance to experience and enjoy a future in the regular world.

Fortunately for me, I eventually married someone who came from a loving and close family. She taught me to accept and express love, and to have faith in myself. In turn, I influenced her to become more adventurous, and to strive for goals that might seem unreachable.

But my real foundation was laid in the Masonic Home. The habits I practice today stem from my training there. I still like dinner at the same time every evening; I still fold and place my socks and shorts neatly in a drawer; I still insist on a schedule that is consistent and predictable.

And I have learned to appreciate what I have, instead of searching for some unattainable fantasy. Mother Downen's story about The House with the Golden Windows taught me the right moral: "What is good and wonderful isn't out there somewhere; your own house is the one with the golden windows."

I had the treasure all the time I was in the Home. It

wasn't a mysterious charter telling of hidden riches. Rather, it was having sweet Mrs. Copeland for a housemother, Hogie for a Scout Master, and gentle, older guys such as Russell Hocks and Bunny Boast being friendly with a young kid.

The real treasures were the marble contests in the Apple Seed, the games of Prisoner's Base, the lightning slides, and the mines filled with bats. They were the bond that formed between Jack and myself when he came down with Scarlet Fever and I signaled to him through the hospital window each day.

Friendship like this lasts forever. Yes, I had the treasure, all the time!

Sister Marie, Brothers Walter and Earl
and Cousin Merle